S0-EGR-803

SMALL
FRUIT AND
VEGETABLE
GARDENS

Jacqueline Heriteau

73031

STERLING PUBLISHING CO., INC.   NEW YORK
Oak Tree Press Co., Ltd. London & Sydney

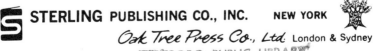

ACKNOWLEDGMENTS

To Elvin McDonald, *House Beautiful* Senior Editor, and Sheila Levine, Popular Library Editor, who played father and mother to this book, my gratitude for their enthusiasm for the concept and their patience with the production. To artist Peter Kalberkamp for the how-to drawings and adept translation of the planting plans, and to Betty Brinhart for the how-to photographs, I am much indebted. Thanks are due as well to the Burpee Seed Company, the Four Winds Growers, the United States Department of Agriculture, the Toro Company. Also to the Armstrong Nurseries, Inc., Ontario, Canada, for photographs and information on special areas of gardening in small spaces, and to the California Redwood Association, which provided the sketches and information for the construction of various containers. A very special thank-you to Maxine Krasnow who somehow deciphered my untidy manuscript and typed it in legible form.

Jacqueline Hériteau
New York, N.Y.

Published by Sterling Publishing Co, Inc.
419 Park Avenue South, New York 10016
Distributed in Australia and New Zealand by Oak Tree Press Co., Ltd.,
P.O. Box J34, Brickfield Hill, Sydney 2000, N.S.W.
Distributed in the United Kingdom and elsewhere in the British Commonwealth
by Ward Lock Ltd., 116 Baker Street, London W 1
Manufactured in the United States of America

Library of Congress Catalog Card No.: 76-1441
Sterling ISBN 0-8069-3072-1 Trade   Oak Tree 7061-2181-3
3073-X Library

To Elvin McDonald, super garden editor, much-loved friend, and the most invariably good person I have ever known.

TABLE OF CONTENTS

INTRODUCTION

NO MATTER WHERE YOU LIVE
YOU CAN GROW YOUR OWN FOOD

You can grow a peach without an orchard and all the tomatoes you can use even if you don't have a single foot of real garden to call your own.

In just a few square feet of outdoor space, you can grow enough fruit and vegetables to make significant saving on the weekly supermarket bill in summer.

The secrets of urban and suburban gardeners who have learned to get good crops from tiny growing spaces are here to show you how you can produce money-saving harvests of delicious, nutritious vegetables and fruits no matter where you live.

Part I

FINDING SPACE FOR FOOD CROPS

Chapter One

LITTLE GARDENS FOR
LUXURIOUS FOODS

The little vegetable and fruit garden is a real money-saver. Tote up your savings the first year on the summer costs of vegetables and especially salad makings, add in the money saved by freezing or storing extras for winter use, and you'll agree.

But perhaps the most appealing use of the little vegetable and fruit garden is to provide luxury items: tender, fresh green asparagus spears in early spring, artichokes, wild strawberries, or big juicy domestic strawberries, raspberries, peaches, your favorite apples, green beans, baby eggplants for cocktail pickling, big Bermuda onions for shish kebabs, buttery Bibb and Boston lettuce, rare varieties of tomatoes and cucumbers—the list is mouth watering and wholesome.

Or use your little garden to grow family specialties—or institute family projects. Peanuts to make your own peanut butter, grapes to make your own jelly, cucumbers to pickle, fruits to preserve and herbs for Christmas giving, catnip for pussy, berries for the freezer, shell beans so the Boston baked beans you make are really from scratch—from the ground up.

The excuses for growing your own are endless, and the pleasure real. Though you may love flowers and grow them for bouquets and drying, you'll find there is even more satisfaction in giving away or setting on the table, foods you have grown yourself—wholesome, nutritious, fresh, delicious.

13

HOW MUCH SPACE DO I NEED?

You can grow food plants in whatever space you have. Mushrooms will grow in a damp, dark basement; many herbs and a few salad plants will grow under grow lights in a sunless room; you can grow miniature gardens of various sizes and shapes on a fire escape (if there's sun), a window ledge, a patio or a terrace. From the smallest urban house lot you can harvest orchard fruits, berries, and supply your household with fresh vegetables during the summer.

Basket grown lettuce will flourish on the patio in the sun.

In a garden as little as 10 by 15 feet you can harvest crops of tomatoes, peppers, Spanish or Bermuda onions, early and late lettuce, squash, green beans, beets, carrots, or turnips, and your favorite herbs.

In an open garden the size of a medium living room (25 by 25 feet), you can grow bush beans, chard, cress, cucumbers, kale, kohlrabi, leaf lettuce, early peas, radishes, scallions, spinach, squash, turnips, late carrots, turnips, celery, onions, parsnips, pumpkins, rutabaga or late turnips, and winter squash—enough to supply a family of four or five with fresh vegetables and salad makings from late spring to autumn, and with some left over to can, freeze, and pickle.

Look at the illustration of the 12 by 18 foot patio garden

and you'll see some of the ways to fit food crops into small spaces.

Tomato growing in sacking or plastic.

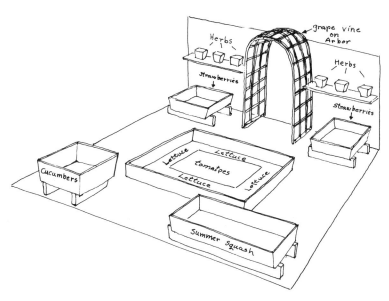

Patio or terrace has room for grapes, herbs, berries, vegetables, and salad makings all grown in containers.

CLIMBERS FIT SMALL SPACES

The grapevines growing over the arbor at the back of a patio take up little space and produce fine crops. Climbing varieties of strawberries are available as well as many species of shell and string beans, peas, squash, cucumbers, and many other vegetables.

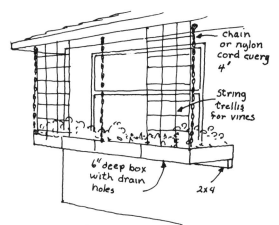

Big window box garden for vegetables.

Window garden extended beyond roof line.

They don't have to climb an arbor; they can climb a mail box, fence, trellised wall, or free-standing stakes, a pole hold-

16

ing a clothesline, or anything offering a rough surface or on which you place wood strips, wire, or string on which the climber's tendrils can wind.

TRY HANGING BASKETS

Plants that require staking but don't grow into tall climbers can be grown in hanging baskets with good results. Actually, almost any plant will grow in a hanging basket but it is pointless to go to the trouble of creating a hanging basket unless the result will be really pretty or unless the harvest will last a while.

The small cocktail variety of tomatoes is attractive grown in hanging baskets and the harvest period will last several weeks. Chives, which can be cut and will grow again, aren't particularly pretty in a hanging basket but you can harvest

Tomatoes flourish in pots and other small containers.

them forever. Small cucumbers are pretty growing in baskets and produce ripe vegetables over a period of time as do the baby eggplants.

ALMOST ANYTHING GROWS IN A POT
OR CONTAINER

You can pot up all of the herbs and set them on sunny window ledges or shelves or outdoor walls. Again, you can grow anything (except perhaps a root vegetable) in a pot but the right type of plant for a pot is one with a long harvest season.

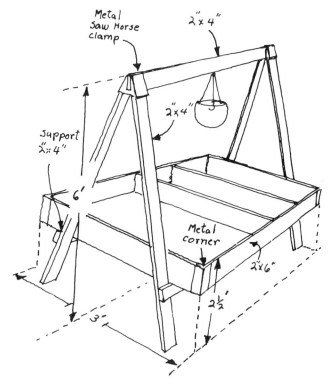

Raised boxes for growing vegetables.

I can't think of a vegetable or a fruit that won't grow in a container of clay, wood, or plastic. Containers can be low flats, flats raised on legs, or big open ones.

Four Winds Growers, in Mission San Jose, bring valencia oranges to fruit in containers of all sizes. This one has been trained in almost formal bonsai form.

Dwarf and semi-dwarf varieties of apples and pears and other orchard fruits will grow and produce excellent crops in large tubs.

For larger gardens, build stepped containers like the one illustrated. This is just one of many variations on the container theme. Railroad ties set into a slope offer similar gardening space.

INVESTIGATE LITTLE SPACES

Once you realize that food plants can grow in containers and small spaces, you can look for growing spaces in the smallest of urban lots with a new viewpoint. A whole orchard of dwarf peaches can grow in what might be a small flower border. All your favorite herbs can be fitted into a spot 2 or 3 feet square. Herbs also grow well between the bricks or flagstones of the path to the street. You can grow a whole salad

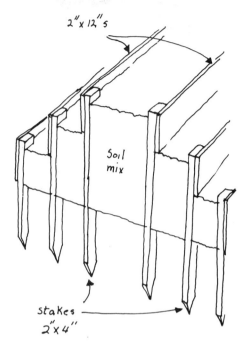

2″ x 12″ s

Soil mix

stakes
2″ x 4″

Stepped garden container for rows of vegetables.

garden in a 12-foot flower bed without sacrificing the appearance of the border. Love fresh green beans? Line the front walkway with a dwarf bush variety—they'll look pretty through the early part of the harvest, and you can replace them with potted petunias when they get tacky. Set four rhubarb plants in a hollow in the lawn—the flowers are especially decorative, the plants perennial.

Look over your domain, however little and unlikely it seems as the home for a lush crop of delicious fresh fruits and vegetables, and you'll be astonished at how much of it can be used to grow food crops.

The plan on this page shows some of the ways a lot of food plants can be fitted into a small landscape.

You can grow a whole orchard of the dwarf Bonanza peaches in a very small space and expect bushels of peaches in 2 or 3 years.

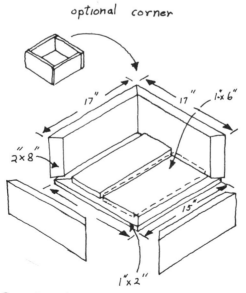

Container for growing dwarf fruit trees.

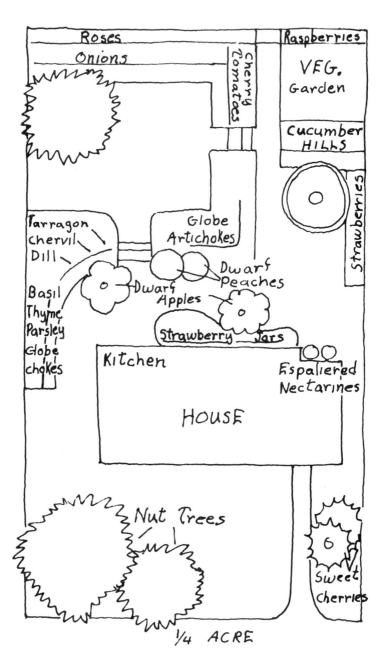

Quarter acre urban house lot can accommodate fruit trees, nut trees, a small vegetable garden, and all the herbs you can use.

TRY THE MINIATURE
VEGETABLES AND FRUITS

Time was when I would have said that corn, which soars to 6 feet and requires lots of room, is the only thing you can't grow gracefully in a small garden, but that is no longer true. Many breeders have produced miniature varieties of corn and other vegetables and fruits, which are small enough to fit into almost any space.

Miniature varieties of vegetables that once were too large for the small garden are now available and make it possible to grow even corn in very limited space. (Photo by J. F. Michajluk.)

Some of these miniature plants are particularly desirable, not because they are so small but also because they ripen quickly. The mini-watermelons and dwarf peaches are examples. Where standard (regular) size fruit trees take from 3 to 6 years to mature real crops, the dwarf and semi-dwarfs bear fruit the second year. (And they would bear in the first year too. However, the tree's future development is harmed if it is allowed to set fruit the first year.)

Watermelon in miniature ripens in July even in cool regions and will fit into a very small garden space. (Photo by J. F. Michajluk.)

DECIDING ON THE SIZE OF THE GARDEN

Once it is clear that you can grow your own vegetables and fruits no matter where you live, the next question is how much of the space you have should be devoted to food plants. And that decision hangs in part on the purpose of your garden.

Will it be a luxury garden? Then make a list of the expensive fruits or vegetables you'd like to grow. Take this list to your landscape, and figure out with the help of the table of vegetable yields how much you can fit in. Will your garden be for special projects? Decide what you want to grow, and see how much will fit and where. A lot of peach trees, or rhubarb, can be worked into existing plantings, but a lot of only one type of plant makes for a monotonous looking garden so try to grow a few different plants rather than a huge quantity of one.

Will yours be an inflation garden? You can turn the whole of your private segment of the outdoors into an inflation-fighting jungle, and the planting plans in the next chapter suggest how.

But if you just want a little garden to take the edge off the budget tremors, look for a sunny open square of soil some-where between 10 by 10 and 25 by 25 feet. Or any rectangular or circular, flat or rolling variation of that theme will do. During the summer, a 10 by 10 feet garden will supply salad makings, herbs, and a few favorite vegetables for a family of two to four. The larger garden will supply everything in the way of vegetables and salad for a family of four and also some left over to freeze and preserve for winter eating.

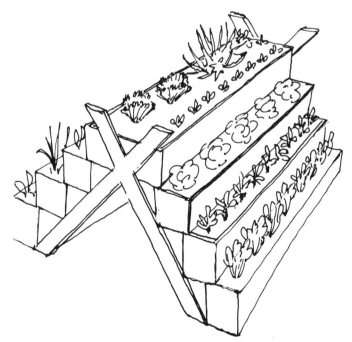

Stepped garden with seedlings.

25

A big vegetable garden that will grow almost everything you can think of in the way of vegetables in sufficient quantity to feed a family of four or five throughout the year is about 50 by 100 feet. A garden that size is really a lot of work. The little garden is much more suitable for most families.

This Table of Yields will give you a notion of how much of what produces what size harvest. Use it as a guide when you are deciding the type and size of garden and how much space it will need.

VEGETABLE YIELDS

Vegetable	Plants per 25 foot row	Yield per 25 foot row	Space between rows (inches)	Space between plants (inches)
Artichokes (perennial)	9 plants	1 bushel	36	36
Asparagus (perennial)	18 plants	12 lbs.	24–48	18
Beans				
bush snap,	⅛ lb.	12 quarts	20–30	3–5
pole snap,	⅛ lb.	1 bushel	30–36	4–6 plants per pole
lima, bush	⅛ lb.	3½ qts.	30–36	4
lima, pole	¼ lb.	5 qts.	30–36	4–6 plants per pole
Beets	¼ oz.	½ bushel	12–18	2–3
Broccoli	12 plants (½ pk. seed)	12–20 heads	20–24	18
Brussels sprouts	12 plants (½ pk. seed)	½–1 bushel	20–24	18
Cabbage	12 plants (½ pk. seed)	12 heads	20–24	18
Carrots	⅛ oz.	½ bushel	20	1–2
Cauliflower	12 plants (½ pk. seed)	12 heads	20–24	18
Celeriac	⅛ pk.	50 roots	20	6
Celery	⅛ pk.	50	20–24	6

Chard, Swiss	¼ oz.	1 bushel	18	4–6
Chicory	¼ pk.	15 lbs.	12	4
Corn				
sweet	⅛ lb.	38 ears	36	8
Indian	⅛ lb.	38 ears	24–36	10–12
popcorn	⅛ lb.	6–7 lbs.	24–36	10–12
Cress, Garden	½ pk.	10 lbs.	24	12
Cucumbers	¼ pk.	38 lbs.	48	4–6
Dandelion (perennial)	¼ pk.	15 lbs.	18	4
Eggplant	¼ pk.	75 fruit	20–30	18
Endive and escarole	¼ pk.	25 lbs.	12	4
Garlic (cloves)	¼ lb.	⅜ bushel	8	3
Gourds	¼ pk.	too much	36	60
Horseradish (perennial)	12 roots	⅜ bushel	24	15
Jerusalem artichoke (perennial)	1–1½ lbs.	1 bushel	36–48	18
Kale	¼ pk.	62 lbs.	12–18	10
Kohlrabi	⅛ oz.	15 lbs.	48	4–6
Leeks	1 pk.	50 plants	10–12	2–3 later 6
Lettuce	½ pk.	25 lbs.	12	2–3
Melons				
cantaloupe	¼ pk.	20–30 fruit	48	8–10
watermelon	½ pk.	75 lbs.	72	36
New Zealand spinach	¼ pk.	2 bushels	18	4–6
Okra	1 pk.	15 qts.	20	15–24
Onion sets	¼ lb.	½ bushel	12	8
Parsley (see herbs) (biennial)	¼ pk.	12 lbs.	18	6–8
Parsnips	1 pk.	¾ bushel	12	3–4
Peas	¼ lb.	½ bushel	20–30	4
Peppers	18 plants	1 bushel	20–24	18

Vegetable Yields (Continued)

Vegetable	Plants per 25 foot row	Yield per 25 foot row	Space between rows (inches)	Space between plants (inches)
Potatoes	1–1½ lbs.	1 bushel	24–36	18
Pumpkins	¼ pk.	75 lbs.	60	60
Radishes	1 pk.	25 bunches	12	1–2
Rhubarb (perennial)	8 roots	too much	36	36
Rutabaga	½ pk.	½ bushel	18	8
Salsify	1 pk.	½ bushel	12	3–4
Shallots	¼ lb.	¼ bushel	21	3
Spinach	¼ oz.	½ bushel	18	6
Squash summer	¼ pk.	30–35 lbs.	24–36	6
winter	¼ pk.	75 lbs.	72	60
Strawberries (perennial)	18 plants	¼–½ qt.	48	18
Sweet potatoes	1–1½ lbs.	1 bushel	24–36	18
Tomatoes	9 plants	38 lbs.	36–48	24-36
Turnips	½ pk.	½ bushel	18	6
Watercress	100	too much	4	3

FRUIT YIELDS

Fruit	Yield	Height (feet)	Distance between rows (feet)	Distance between plants	Pollination
Apple, Dwarf	1–2 bushels	8–10	Allow 10 x 10		Cross-pollination required
Semi-dwarf	2–3 bushels	12–15	Allow 10 x 20		Cross-pollination required

Blackberry	1¼ qt.	6–7	6–7	3	
Blueberry	4 qts.	10–15	8–10	4–5	Cross-pollination improves yield
Cherry, Standard Sour	1–2 bushels	20–25	Allow 16 x 16		Self-pollinating
Semi-dwarf Sweet	1–2 bushels	12–15	Allow 10 x 20		Cross-pollination required
Grapes	15–30 lbs.	up to 50	7	7	Some require cross-pollination
Nectarine	As above	As above	Allow 10 x 20		Self-pollinating
Peach, Dwarf	1–2 bushels	8–10	Allow 10 x 10		Most self-pollinating
Semi-dwarf	2–3 bushels	12–15	Allow 10 x 20		Self-pollinating
Pear, Dwarf	1–2 bushels	8–10	Allow 10 x 10		Cross-pollination required
Semi-dwarf	2–3 bushels	12–15	Allow 10 x 20		Cross-pollination required
Plum	2–4 bushels	20–25	Allow 16 x 16		Cross-pollination required
Semi-dwarf	1–2 bushels	12–15	Allow 10 x 20		Most require cross-pollination
Raspberry	1½ qts.	6–8	6–7	3	
Strawberry	1 qt.	½	3–4	1½	A few require cross-pollination

Chapter Two

PLANTING PLANS FOR LITTLE GARDENS

A planting plan is the key to efficient seed buying and to big yields in little spaces. One of the most common first-season complaints of gardeners new to food growing is that they were flooded with squash or lettuce or beans or tomatoes, that too much of one thing was ready to pick at the same time—and then there was none. "I ate beans until they came out the children's ears," is typical. It doesn't have to happen.

It stands to reason that if you plant a whole packet of bean seeds the same hour, water and maintain them all the same way, they are all likely to bear crops at the same time. Actually, they don't. Depending on the soil, each plant ripens a few beans every other day or so for a period of 2 or 3 weeks so you need a 6- to 10-foot row of bean plants in order to gather enough for a meal in one picking. You can plant fewer and collect the beans over a period of several days, but they are most delicious when first picked.

Ideally, popular staples like beans which will mature throughout the summer weeks (as opposed to peas which mature only in spring) should ripen in waves. To achieve that happy state, you plant one crop in spring (late April or May in New England), another crop 3 or so weeks later, and another crop 3 weeks after that. Then you will have green beans from July on through the warm weather in September. This is called "succession planting."

Another way to create successions, or waves, is to plant varieties that mature at different dates. Tomatoes are a good example: Tiny Tim and cocktail tomatoes when set out as soon as danger of night frosts is past will ripen in good soil toward the end of July, or even sooner. The larger mini-tomatoes will ripen about 2 weeks later, and the standard sizes begin to come in toward the end of August (in New England). Some special varieties of the standards, the lovely yellow tomatoes and some of the pinks, come in later. By planting a few of each variety at the same time, you'll have some tomatoes all summer long.

DOUBLING AND TRIPLING
GARDEN YIELDS

Another form of succession planting is to sow vegetables that ripen in mid-season where a crop that ripened early and has been harvested has left an empty row in the garden. Start with radishes, which can be planted as soon as frost is out of the ground and mature 3 to 6 weeks later. Then plant cocktail tomatoes in their place and follow with a final crop of lettuce. The lettuce, planted in August, will be ready to pick in September. A two-crop succession planting is easier on the gardener: radishes followed by tomatoes which will still be maturing in September is typical.

By well thought-out succession planting, the smallest garden can be made to yield a wonderful variety of vegetables. So, as you work out a planting plan for your little garden, be sure you keep all the rows occupied from the time the frost is out of the ground until the frosts return. The table shows the number of days to maturity for the most popular vegetables. Use it to figure out which late or midseason crops can be planted when the earliest crops are out of the ground.

Days to Maturity

Vegetable	Approximate days to maturity
Artichokes (perennial)	second season
Asparagus (perennial)	second or third year
Beans	
bush, snap	55–65 days
pole	65 days
lima, bush	65–75 days
lima, pole	12–14 weeks
Beets	early 45 days late 80 days
Broccoli	plants, 50-60 days seeds, 80-100 days
Brussels sprouts	plants, 60-70 days seeds, 95 days
Cabbage	40–90 days
Carrots	plants, 65–75 days seeds, 80–100 days
Cauliflower	plants, 50-60 days seeds, 80-90 days
Celeriac	120 days
Celery	120 days
Chard, Swiss	55–60 days
Chicory	112 days
Corn	
sweet	75 days
Indian	105 days
popcorn	90–105 days
Cress, Garden	20 days
Cucumbers	50 days
Dandelion (perennial)	second season
Eggplant	60–75 days
Endive and escarole	65–90 days

Days to Maturity (Continued)

Vegetable	Approximate days to maturity
Garlic (cloves)	125 days
Gourds	100 days
Jerusalem artichoke (perennial)	120 days
Kale	56–75 days
Kohlrabi	48–60 days
Leeks	130 days
Lettuce	40–90 days
Melons	
cantaloupe	70 days
watermelon	70–85 days
New Zealand spinach	60–70 days
Okra	56 days
Onion sets	110 days
Parsley (biennial)	120 days
Parsnips	95-150 days
Peas	early 60 days
	late 80 days
Peppers	60–80 days
Potatoes	80–100 days
Pumpkins	100–120 days
Radishes	early 20 days
	late 60 days
Rhubarb (perennial)	second season
Rutabaga	85–90 days
Salsify	120 days
Spinach,	40–50 days
Squash	
summer	45–50 days
winter	90–110 days

Vegetable	Approximate days to maturity
Strawberries (perennial)	second season
Sweet potatoes	120–150 days
Tomatoes	52–80 days
Turnips	early 35 days late 60 days

WHEN DO THE FRUIT PLANTS MATURE CROPS

Both the orchard fruits (like pears and peaches) and the bramble fruits (berries) are available in varieties that bear at different times of the season. With careful planning, you can have some fresh fruit all season long.

To locate fruit for your garden that will provide a succession of crops, ask the Agricultural Extension Service and the local garden supply centers for recommended species, check the harvest dates of the various varieties of each species, then plant varieties whose crops succeed each other.

By careful selection, you can have apples from July through fall, pears from July/August through late fall, plums, peaches, and nectarines from July through October, cherries from June through mid-August, strawberries from June through September, raspberries from July to late September, grapes from August through October, and blueberries from June through late September.

As a rule of thumb, the berry plants are harvested the *second* season after planting. Though they will produce the blossoms from which fruit develop the first year, it is generally recommended that this first season fruit be prevented from developing. This is true of the bramble fruits, like raspberries, as well as of strawberries.

The berry varieties called "everbearer" produce fruit in quantity early or late in the season, and some fruit throughout the rest of the season. Some growers recommend that their varieties be allowed to set fruit the first year.

Apples, pears, peaches, nectarines, sweet and sour cherries, and plums—the orchard fruits—are today available in dwarf and semi-dwarf varieties—low-growing trees that are quick to mature. The Yield table shows that they produce harvests well worth having the second or third year after planting and will bear for years to come. Not all the standard-size orchard fruits bear so quickly, which makes the dwarfs and semi-dwarfs doubly desirable for the small garden.

INTERCROPPING

Another way to increase garden yields is to plant between plants. This is called "intercropping." Glance back at the Days to Maturity table and you will see that some vegetables produce their crops in as little as 3 weeks, while others require as much as 5 months. By combining plantings of the low-growing, quick-to-mature vegetables such as radishes and lettuce with plantings of slower, taller species such as late Brussels sprouts, one row can be made to yield two crops simultaneously. The second, or slow crop, need not be tall. Combinations of quick-growing and slow-growing seeds will produce plants of similar size. Either radishes or garden cress, which grow and mature quickly, can be planted at the same time and in the same row with carrots, which grow and mature slowly. The carrots won't be ready to pick until at least 6 weeks after the radishes are out.

In one row you can grow tall vegetables with low-growing vegetables. Cucumber or pumpkin vines are often planted at the feet of corn. Another good pair is pole beans with onions. The only caution is that the low-growers must receive a share of sunlight. Pumpkins are one of the few which succeed in a somewhat shaded location.

HOW TO MAKE A PLANTING PLAN

Planting plans generally require lots of revision. You tend to discard one favorite for another as you gather information and work towards a garden that uses its space continuously and productively with succession plantings and intercropping. Make rough drafts until you are sure of what is going where. I draw mine on draft paper using each square to represent 1

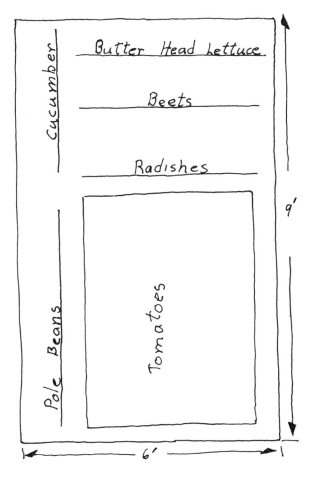

Single crop mini garden.

foot of garden space. Work on a large sheet so you can make everything clear, and be sure the proportions of the squares accurately represent the number of feet in the length and in the width of the garden.

The illustrations explain better than words what a planting plan is.

The single-crop mini-garden, which includes cucumbers, pole beans (a long-season crop), tomatoes, early lettuce, beets (a long-season crop), and radishes, is a no-sweat garden that will have a little to offer for dinner almost every week of

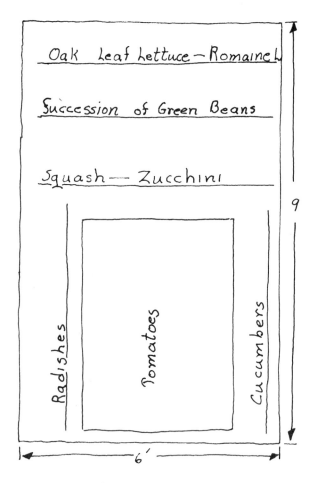

Double crop mini garden.

the season. However, the same space can be used much more efficiently. Look at the double-crop mini-garden, and you'll see how succession planting and intercropping have been used to increase the harvest in this garden.

Little Garden 1, which is only 9 by 12 feet, grows cucumbers, pole beans, squash, peppers, tomatoes, early carrots, late beets, onions, green beans, oak leaf and romaine lettuce, along with a few plants of everbearer strawberries. It uses every inch of growing space all season long.

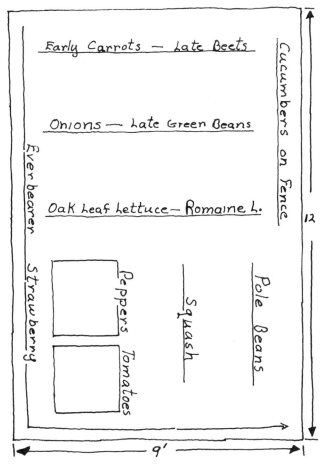

Little garden 1.

Little Garden 2, which is 12 by 15 feet, has a whole produce-counter full of vegetables and salad makings to offer throughout the season. You could find space for a few more, if you wanted to, and could edge the garden with everbearer wild strawberries.

Little garden 2.

Use these planting plans in conjunction with the Yield and Days to Maturity tables to work out succession planting and intercropping programs that will give your garden the utmost yield for its size.

PLANNING CONTAINER GARDENS

The planting plans here suggest what can be planted in the small space of a container garden. Beets, carrots, and turnips, crops whose roots are the edible portion, take a fair amount of

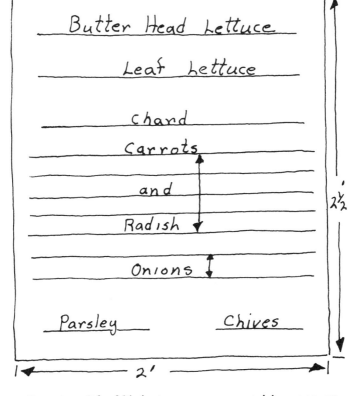

Container 2 by 2½ feet can grow a surprising amount.

space and aren't particularly suited to container gardening. If they're among your favorites, go ahead and plant them in boxed or raised beds. All manner of salad greens and specialties such as strawberries, rhubarb, chives, and herbs are well-suited to containerized beds, and so are tomatoes, sweet peppers, and the big, sweet Bermuda onions.

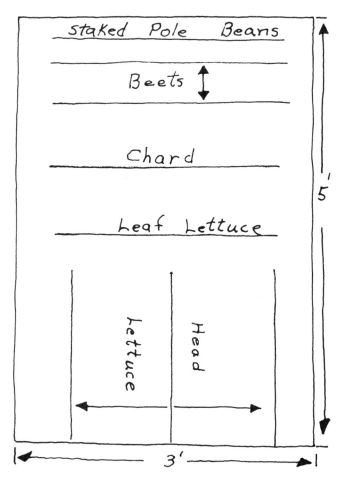

Container garden 3 by 5 feet yields beets, beans, chard for boilings greens, and lettuce. Plant oak leaf lettuce for an early crop and when summer heat comes, replace the oak leaf with romaine lettuce.

PLANNING A FLOWER BORDER WITH HERBS AND VEGETABLES

With careful planning, you can hide a little food garden right in your flower beds. (You could plant one in with the foundation plantings around the house, too. However, most foundation plantings include many evergreens, and soils suited to evergreens are a shade too acid for most food plants. Highbush blueberries, which thrive in acid soil, can be planted right in with foundation plantings if you like.)

By "hide" I meant blend. Many food plants are decorative enough to be grown with ornamental plants. The planting plans for mixed vegetable and flower gardens will suggest some ideas.

Before you embark on your own plan for a mixed food and flower border, remember that many of the food plants die when the harvest is over. You can use this fact to your advantage by planting seeds for flowers that will begin to fill up the row when the food plant dies and is ready to be pulled out.

The planting plan for a mixed border (16 by 8 feet) includes a row of 10 asparagus plants, which will produce enough asparagus spears for a small family once the plants have matured.

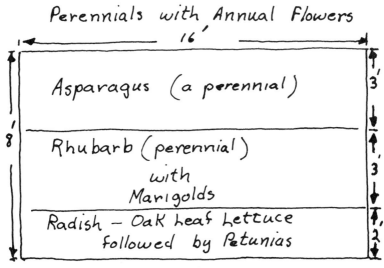

Perennials with annual flowers.

Asparagus is a perennial, one of the few among vegetables. In the year or two you may wait for the plants to mature, the row will be filled with feathery asparagus fern (the kind florists give you with roses) and once the bed has matured and the spring cutting season is over, the bed will fill with tall feathers of asparagus fern that will last through the summer season. You can cut them for bouquets or just let them wave in the breezes. They make a beautiful backdrop for any border. In the first years, while you are waiting for the bed to mature, you can plant tall flowers, such as sunflowers, between the asparagus plants to fill the bed. Or, in early spring the row can be made to yield a crop of radish and early lettuce.

The second row of this plan contains marigolds with three rhubarb plants in their midst. Rhubarb branches are picked in spring, and after the picking season, the plant develops great tall creamy white clusters of flowers that are very pretty. The front of the bed will be filled in summer with a froth of dwarf ruffled petunias, either in colors or in white. Before it is time to plant the petunias (use started seedlings), you can grow garden cress (tastes a little like watercress), a crop that goes in and comes out in 4 weeks, or early lettuce or radishes, or any other of the quick, early spring crops.

The planting plan for an annual mixed border of vegetables, herbs, and flowers (16 by 8 feet) has four tomato plants at

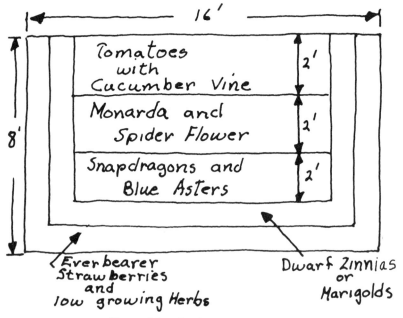

Vegetables, herbs, and flowers.

44

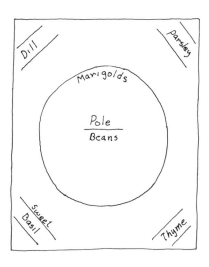

Square Planting
4' x 4'

Dill

Parsley

Marigolds

Pole
Beans

Sweet
Basil

Thyme

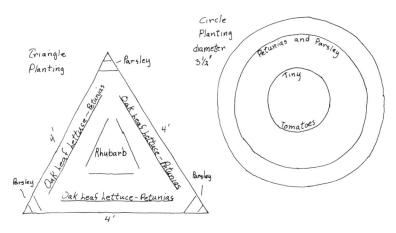

Triangle
Planting

Parsley

Oak leaf Lettuce-Petunias

Oak leaf Lettuce-Petunias

4'

4'

Rhubarb

Parsley

Parsley

Oak leaf Lettuce-Petunias

4'

Circle
Planting
diameter
3½'

Petunias and Parsley

Tiny

Tomatoes

Small circular, triangular, or square plantings combining vege-tables and flowers can be spotted throughout the landscape where there is a bit of space.

the back with cucumbers at their feet. In summer, the row in front of the tomatoes is filled with monarda (bee balm), a perennial, and spider flowers. The row in front of the monarda

45

will bloom in summer with snapdragon spears in white (keep them cut for bouquets to encourage bloom), and later in the summer, the white of the snapdragons will be complimented by the blue of the asters.

Snapdragons and asters are both annuals, so this row can be planted in early lettuce, radishes, or garden cress as soon as the frost is out of the ground. Or you can grow succession plantings of green beans here instead of flowers.

Around the snapdragons and up the sides of the border, 12-by 16-inch tall herbs have been planted along with little ever-bearer wild strawberries, which will yield a few fruit throughout summer for topping ice cream and desserts. Behind the strawberries are planted mixed colors of dwarf zinnias in dusky shades, or marigolds.

Another way to grow flowers and vegetables together is in spot plantings like the three small plans shown here. In the circle, the center is filled with a tall-growing cocktail tomato, staked on a tripod. Parsley plants mixed with medium-height petunias fill the bed.

In the triangle two rhubarb plants are surrounded by oak leaf lettuce, which is planted in early spring and is pretty well finished by June. When the oak leaf is fading away, the bed will fill with petunias (or dwarf zinnias or dwarf marigolds). Parsley fills the corners.

The square spot planting has two pole beans in the center. Choose a variety with colorful flowers and a long harvest season. At its feet are herbs and dwarf marigolds in bright yellow.

The little spot beds can be free form, too. Spotted here and there in the landscape, where soil is available and there is plenty of light, they're a delight to look at and harvest from.

Part II

BASICS FOR THE FOOD GARDEN

Chapter Three

SOILS—WATERING-WEEDING-
MULCHING-FERTILIZING-TOOLS

Garden literature calls for mysterious ingredients and the names alone used to scare me half to death. The most often seen is the word "loam." Then there are the adjectives that go with it—"good, garden" loam. Another one is "friable," which also turns up as "friability." Equally mysterious is "soil pH." Then there are calls for "well-rotted manure" (which never seems available) and "humus," sometimes seen as "humusy soil."

The words are scary because they leave you feeling there are hazardous variables you don't know anything about that are going to keep your garden from growing. The reason gardening writers use the words so often is that they apply to the condition of the soil ideal for plant growth. If the soil conditions are off, plants are just like cars trying to operate on the wrong kind of fuel—you may get them to go a few miles, but you won't get a long, superhighway trip out of the tankful. If the soil isn't right, you won't get a good crop from a small garden space, or a container garden.

GETTING THE SOIL RIGHT

Soil will produce bumper crops if 1) structure or composition is right, 2) fertility is high, 3) pH balance is correct for the plants growing in it.

Structure or *composition* refers to the particles that make up the soil. Vegetable and fruit plants grow best in the soil type called "loam." It is composed of about ⅓ clay, ⅓ sand, and ⅓ humus. Potting soils sold commercially are "loam" and contain these three elements in about equal parts. The soil in your backyard, on the other hand, may be sandy loam—soil with a largely sandy content—clay loam, soil with too much clay, or (rarely) pure humus.

Humus, the magic word in the organic gardener's lexicon, is organic matter that has decomposed into a light, fluffy stuff, like peat moss. Its virtue is that it lightens soil and, above all, holds lots of moisture. Clay is rich in nutrients—building blocks for plant growth. Sand aerates the soil.

To grow well, plants must have the nutrients from the clay in the soil—but clay particles are very fine (that's why clay packs into an unbreakable lump when balled). So they also need the air spaces provided by the coarse particles of the sand. Sand, however, absorbs no water, lets it all leach through (a fact we rely on to avoid soggy soils filled with stagnant water) —so the plants need humus in soil to retain the moisture essential to their unchecked growth.

Loam soils, then, hold lots of air and moisture. In this moisture the nutrients the plants require are held in somewhat soluble state. Nutrients reach plants by means of millions of little hairlike cells that grow on the roots and absorb dissolved nutrients and carry them through the plant system. In light, airy, loamy soil, these cells can expand easily and operate at maximum efficiency. Good garden loam is worth the effort it may take to create it because it will grow lush plants that produce bumper crops.

HOW TO RECOGNIZE GOOD GARDEN LOAM

Test the soil available to you this way: on a day when the soil is damp, but not moist, pick up a handful and pack it with both hands as though you were making a snowball. If the soil won't adhere to make a ball, it has too large a sand content. If it will ball easily and it will crumble easily under slight pressure, it is well-balanced loam. If it won't crumble easily, it has a high clay content. Soils that ball and crumble easily under pressure are called "friable."

TURNING POOR SOIL INTO LOAM

The way to correct soil structure, turn it into "good garden loam," is to add whatever the missing element or elements may be. To soils too high in clay content, we add humus and sand. Not just any sand will do. Builders work with a type of sand called "sharp sand." Under a magnifying glass, the particles show jagged edges that create air spaces when closely packed. The grains are smaller than gravel and different from fill sand. Sea sand may be "sharp" in structure but it also contains salts which may be harmful. It must be washed completely free of such salts before it can be added to garden soil, and that is an impractical task unless you are using a very small amount. If you are adding sand to a big garden, buy "sharp" sand and dig it in. Garden supply centers sell it in small quantities. Construction suppliers sell it by the "yard," a measure resembling a small truckful.

Humus, decomposed organic matter, is available in a number of forms. The various types of peat moss sold everywhere are the forms most commonly used. Woodland soil is often almost pure humus for the top several inches. Decomposed, or well-rotted manures, are humus. Unlike other forms of humus, which generally have a few of the nutrients needed for soil fertilizer, rotted manure is extremely fertile. (See below.) Compost and decomposed seaweeds are other forms of fertile humus.

To soils too high in sand, we add humus to improve structure. To soil too high in humus (exceedingly rare) we add purchased loam.

TESTING TO SEE WHAT ELEMENTS ARE MISSING

How much of what do you add? If you want to be absolutely sure of the answer, take advantage of the help offered by the Agricultural Extension Service. Local branches are maintained at most State Universities. The Service will test your soil in most states for free or a small fee, and recommend solutions. The Service is not, as generally supposed, intended only to help professional farmers—it is also meant to help the home gardener. You'll find a list of Extension Service addresses in the Appendix. Dig a small plug of soil from the garden area you are planning to use and send it to the local Service with a request for information on measures to take to make it into loam for food crops.

Or do this: cover a test patch of damp, but not wet, soil about 2 feet square with a 1-inch layer of the element or elements the snowball test suggests are missing. With a trowel or a spading fork, mix the soil thoroughly to a depth of 18 inches and try the snowball test again with this new mixture.

Keep adding the missing element or elements in 1-inch layers until the snowball test shows the soil is friable. Keep a record of how many inches you have added of each element and measure the surface of the soil to be corrected. Give this information to the garden supply center when ordering the missing materials and let them figure out how much sand or humus is needed.

Dig these delivered materials, just as you did the additives in the test patch, into the soil to be improved to a depth of 18 inches, and mix the soil as thoroughly (almost) as a batch of pie dough. It is hard work only if you are correcting a vast expanse, but even if it is hard work, it will pay off for years to come.

SOIL FERTILITY AND ADDING FERTILIZERS

A rich soil, a fertile soil, is soil loaded with the nutrients necessary for plant growth. You can't tell whether soil is fertile or not by its color or feel—you can tell by the way things now growing on it look. If the growth it supports is richly green, stalwart, and lush, it probably is a fertile soil. If the growth is pale green, leggy, spindly, it may be missing important nutrients.

The three basics in fertile soil are nitrogen, phosphorus, and potash. The "complete fertilizers" contain all three. Nitrogen is called the leaf maker. Plants short of nitrogen are stunted and have small, pale-green leaves. Phosphorus (phosphates) is called the root maker. Plants short of phosphate are stunted and have poorly developed roots. Potash is called the flower maker, and when the crop is a fruit or a vegetable (non-leafy) it governs the size of the harvest. Plants short of potash have weak stems, and the flowers that precede the fruit are small and poorly colored. Potash influences plant resistance to disease, and is essential for a healthy garden.

In the good old days when well-rotted manure, a superb

fertilizer, was available to dig into every home garden, no one paid much attention to how much of which of the three main nutrients the garden needed. Manure is a complete fertilizer, nature's way, and it is humus as well. Today, we more often must use chemical fertilizers. The local Extension Service will analyze your soil and report how much of each nutrient it needs to be in balance for the production of food crops. When the Agricultural Extension Service tells you what to do, you feel more secure, but you can analyze the soil yourself with one of the many soil testing kits sold commercially, and come up with the right answers. Or, you can ask a gardening neighbor whose soil is probably similar to yours which fertilizer he uses, and try that.

If you are buying potting soil or loam from the local garden center, rather than creating loam from backyard soil, ask the salesman which fertilizer he recommends for the soil he is selling. It may need none for the first go-round of planting. In Section III are instructions for adding fertilizers to each type of food plant during the growing season.

The chemical fertilizers called "complete fertilizers" include the three elements in various ratios to each other. Descriptive labels, such as 5-10-5 or 1-5-5, refer to the proportion of each nutrient: nitrogen, phosphorus, potash, in that order. To fertilize soil for a vegetable garden dig fertilizer in at a rate of 50 pounds for each 2,500 square feet of garden space.

A more expensive way to fertilize is to dig in purchased, dried, bagged sheep manure (less acid I find than cow manure), or bagged cow manure, at the rate recommended.

Or—if available—dig in lots of well-rotted manure from the local horse stable or farmyard. I prefer the latter, but have rarely been able to get it.

If this approach to fertilizing seems casual as compared to my views on improving soil structure, there's a reason for it. While fertile soil is essential for continued good harvests, without good soil structure, the fertilizers won't be as effective as they should be. Soil less rich in fertilizers but excellent in composition does more for plants than fertilized soil that is so heavy (clay) the plants can't grow, and so sandy they are always short of water.

If you have added lots and lots of humus or compost (see below) to correct composition, should you also add dried or rotted manures? You can, but what you should do is add the dried or rotted manures or compost, counting them as humus,

53

and deducting from the amount of humus required.

While most food plants require similar proportions of nutrients, certain plants have specific needs. These are described in the planting instructions given in Section III.

pH, ACIDITY, AND ALL

pH is another of the magic words we see a lot, especially today when so much emphasis is on organic (which I call common sense) gardening. pH stands for "potential of hydrogen," and the relative acidity or alkalinity of soil is always expressed in terms of pH: neutral is pH 7. Lower readings (pH 6.5) indicate increasing acidity, and higher readings (pH 7.2) increasing alkalinity.

It makes me uncomfortable to generalize, but I'll go out on a limb and say that most American soils have a pH of between 6 and 7. Food plants like slightly acid soils with pH between 6 and 6.8. Why does it matter? Well, because the pH of the soil determines to an important degree the availability of many plant nutrients. In other words, even in fertile loam, plants can have problems if the acidity range is unfavorable.

How can you tell what the pH of your soil is? The Agricultural Extension Service will give you a sure reading, or you can test it yourself with a soil-testing kit. Or, look at the wild lands in your area: if evergreens and oaks flourish, the soil is on the acid side. If not, it's probably in the range of pH 6 to 7.

Soils used for growing crops or lawns year after year become increasingly acid. That's why we lime lawns periodically. Lime "sweetens" soil and most soils in which vegetables are grown need an application of lime every 3 or 4 years.

Soils that are too "sweet" for the plants scheduled to be grown in them (blueberries are one of the few food plants that must have a soil that is distinctly acid) can be acidified by the addition of ammonium sulfate. The rate at which either lime or ammonium sulphate should be added depends on your soil's pH reading.

If you buy loam, specify that it is to be used to grow food and the soil you get will probably have a pH reading suitable for your crops. If you are going to work with the soil in your backyard, make the effort necessary to get the pH right—lime

54

the soil every few years, as you would your lawn, and check the pH annually. This is especially important if you are planning to farm organically using organic mulches and compost.

"ORGANIC GARDENING": WHAT AND WHY?

"Organic gardening" is the way we used to garden before we went overboard on chemicals. Organic gardeners use natural vegetable and mineral materials and their derivatives to improve soil structure and fertility and keep track of pH. They do not use chemicals—either fertilizers or pesticides. Instead, they encourage the plant's natural allies—birds, beneficial insects (Chapter Ten). They believe they grow more nutritious and successful gardens the organic way.

My approach is middle-of-the-road organic—that is, when I can't handle a problem the organic way, I go the chemical route.

COMPOST

The fertile humus that organic gardeners consider magical fertilizer is "compost," fluffy black stuff that looks like soil and feels like a cross between fine soil and humus. Compost is the product of the decomposition of organic matter of all sorts. Organic matter includes leaves, seaweed, grass clippings, soft prunings, straw, hay, sawdust, weeds, plants, vegetable refuse from the kitchen—vegetation of any kind.

The basic method for making compost is to layer together organic matter and soil, with or without lime and fertilizers, and leave the pile to chemistry and weather which together, over a period of time, will cause the heap to decompose into "compost." Books much larger than this one have been written about how to make compost that is tremendously fertile and in good pH balance. But, given 1 to 3 years, whether or not it is layered with soil and babied with additives, organic matter will become good, valuable compost. Obviously a whole tree trunk in a dry climate will take longer to decompose than will a fern leaf in a moist, hot climate.

The most common method of composting is to build a container, a structure 3-, 4-, or 5-feet square (see illustration), and layer in it organic refuse and soil (with a handful each of lime

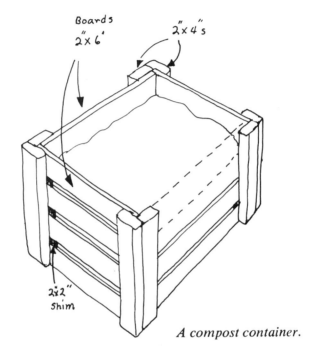

A compost container.

and fertilizer per layer). A box like this one makes a rather neat place in which to pile garden cleanings (as long as they aren't diseased) like weeds, leaves, prunings, as well as garbage (no bones, please). To decompose quickly, the materials require warmth and moisture. The surface of the pile should be concave to catch and hold rain water—and if there's no rain, you must wet it every few weeks. The materials will turn to compost even more quickly and certainly more evenly if you turn the pile every month, mixing it thoroughly.

Not everyone has room for a compost pile this size and lots of us, including me, are making compost in super-large garbage cans and in those giant plastic bags. Making compost in smaller quantities makes handling the materials much easier—especially the turning of the pile.

Fallen leaves are the most readily available organic ingredient for compost for most urban and suburban gardeners. A shredder (either attached to the lawn mower, or a unit such as the one illustrated), which finely grinds the organic materials

Shredder is the one piece of heavy equipment most garden owners wish they had because it cuts up organic matter of all sorts making it ready for quick composting. This 3½ hp model has a dual blade action that cuts lawn debris volume 80 to 90 percent, shreds leaves and vegetable garden discards to a fine, rich mulch. (Courtesy The Toro Company.)

before they go to the composting heap, speeds the decomposition process tremendously, and is one piece of heavy equipment gardeners in small places long for.

To make compost or not to make compost is an individual decision. The value of compost, however, isn't open to question. It is the best humus there is.

WATERING NEEDS FOR SMALL GARDENS

The moisture requirements of food plants depend in part on their containers.

Plants growing in containers need more frequent watering than those growing in the ground. The rule of thumb for container watering is to water whenever the top layer of the soil is distinctly dry. In hot, dry spells in midsummer, this probably means every day. In spring and autumn, container plants probably require watering every 3 or 4 days. Plants in very large plastic or metal containers will require watering less often than plants in small, porous containers made of wood or clay.

Plants growing in the ground require watering about once a week. If it doesn't rain, the job becomes yours.

When you water, water thoroughly. It takes a surprising amount of time for most watering units to get moisture down to the main root systems of many food plants—which are 6 to 8 inches below the soil surface. Measure the amount of water your sprinkler puts down in an hour by setting a glass jar in its watering range for 60 minutes. Between 1 and 1½ inches of water in the jar means moisture penetrating to 6 or 7 inches. Then you can gauge how long your sprinkler should be left on at each watering.

Plants growing in mulched soil will require watering less often than those that have no protective blanket.

MULCHING AND WEEDING

One of the advantages of container gardens is that there's very little weeding to do, and what there is of it is easy.

Weeding is one of the worst of all chores when you are growing food plants in the ground. One of the best ways to avoid weeds is to cover every inch of garden surface with a mulch. A mulch is simply a blanket of organic matter that keeps light and air away from the soil it covers.

Some weeds inevitably are waiting to sprout the day after

you plant an outdoor garden. If you keep these under control, and never let them go to seed, each subsequent year there will be fewer weeds to deal with. The classic way of weeding is to hoe daily between garden rows. A New England way of avoiding weeds later in the summer is to plant vegetables so closely together the tops meet over the soil between rows, cutting off the light without which weeds can't flourish.

My favorite methods for avoiding weeds is to mulch heavily with an organic material—compost, half-decomposed leaves, spoiled straw, or seaweed or with black plastic sheets. Black plastic isn't very pretty in the garden, but it does exactly what a mulch is supposed to do.

The advantage of putting an organic mulch on the garden is that the underside decomposes into humus which can be dug into the soil the following year before planting time.

There are two ways to go about mulching a small garden patch. The first is to plant the seeds, cover the spaces between plantings with mulch, and when the seedings have sprouted in a week or two, add more mulch right up to the plant stems.

The other way is to cover the whole garden with mulch, then part the mulch in straight rows to leave space for the plantings. Either works well. I prefer to plant, then mulch. It seems to me that the soil warms more quickly where there is no mulch and the seeds come up faster. However, this means that I have to keep the weeds under control while I am waiting for the seeds to grow.

Keeping weeding to a minimum is only one of the many advantages in mulching a garden. Mulches keep soil moisture in, protect plants from the effects of lesser droughts, and lessen the frequency with which the garden needs watering.

TOOLS FOR THE SMALL GARDEN

If you have any sort of outdoor garden, you already have on hand most of the equipment needed for food gardening in small spaces. The basic tools I use include the following:

A square-ended hoe and a pointed hoe for planting and cultivating the soil.

A rake for smoothing the soil.

A spading fork, which is what I use for digging soil. It's lighter than a spading shovel and handles soil that has tree and shrub roots with less effort on my part.

A wooden plank to walk on between rows of cultivated soil. The plank distributes your weight and avoids compacting the soil.

Two 6-inch pegs with pointed ends, joined by a long, sturdy cotton string: one peg set in each end of a row, with the string stretched between, creates a planting guide for seeding straight rows.

A sturdy trowel (don't buy bargain equipment—it breaks in weeks) for digging seedlings and for making transplanting holes.

A large plastic bucket to hold water and starter solutions for the transplanting of seedlings.

A watering device whose throw-span will cover the whole garden. Rain-making types of the sort used by garden supply centers are expensive, but worth the investment because they do the job well and last a long time. These do a good job on patios and terraces with many plantings and in the open garden.

Optional: Wheelbarrow for toting it all. Whether or not you need a barrow will depend on the size of your garden. Some kind of toting device encourages the gardener to keep things together.

For harvesting, I use a large flattish basket.

ROTOTILLER

Do you need a rototiller? A rototiller is a blessing if you have a large garden, or a back that makes digging or turning soil difficult. It is more useful for a food garden than for a flower garden, because flower gardens usually have many perennials (plants that come up year after year, and can't be dug up) whereas food plants are almost all annuals that should be turned back into the soil each fall.

If you decide to buy a rototiller, don't use it to dig under the sod where you are establishing a new garden. Many of the

*A rototiller is useful for the medium to large vegetable garden:
use it in the fall to dig up and fluff the soil; and in spring to
prepare the vegetable garden for seeding.*

weeds growing in sod propagate from the smallest of root cuttings—and as the rototiller chops the sod into the soil, it is
putting thousands of fresh weed cuttings into the garden.
Instead, lift the sod off by hand (compost it), then rototill the
garden.

Chapter Four

CHOOSING SEEDS AND STARTING SEEDLINGS

Most vegetables are grown from seed by the home gardener. The exceptions are artichokes and asparagus. (These can, of course, be grown from seed but it is easier to buy plants.) Most fruits are grown from plants or small trees. Among the few exceptions are melons, which are started from seed in the vegetable garden.

Seeds are sold by hardware stores, dime stores, and supermarkets. Garden supply centers sell seeds as well as fruit trees and started seedlings. Farmers generally buy seeds from farm supply centers in packets of large quantity. Their prices are usually a little lower and the quality very good. Mail order suppliers, garden catalogs are mailed in January or February and offer fruit plants as well as vegetable seeds in packets of various sizes.

Great big packets of seeds lure the possessor of the small garden into planting too many seeds per square foot. If he/she can't (as I often can't) bear to thin them to give each plant space enough to mature in, the harvest will be poor.

SEED VARIETIES

Seeds are offered in several "varieties," each with its own specially desirable characteristics. There are dwarf varieties, for instance, of pumpkins, watermelons, and corn, meant for small gardens. There are also "early," "midseason," and "late" varieties.

Early varieties are those which when planted early in the season will usually bear a crop quickly. This means you can harvest them and plant a new crop in the cleared space.

Midseason varieties often have been bred to withstand heat and usually are finished (that is, harvested, and the row free for the new planting) toward the end of summer.

Late varieties usually go into the ground late in the growing season (July or August) and mature in early or mid-fall. In most areas of America, you can plant three sowings of carrots —an "early" crop, a "midseason" crop, and a "late" crop which can be left in the ground until it freezes. In some areas this can be left in the ground through winter and harvested in spring.

The first decision to be made, then, in selecting seeds is the planting date intended—is it to be an early, midseason, or late crop? Chapter Two discussed "succession planting" and "intercropping," methods used to grow several crops in one row. You should consult that chapter and make a planting plan before selecting seed.

There are other considerations in selecting seeds. Certain varieties of each vegetable are recommended for the "home garden." This means they are tops in flavor. Plants meant for commercial gardening have been bred to keep and transport well and usually do not have the flavor or texture of the home garden varieties. Varieties described as good for both home garden and garden stand sale fall somewhere between these two types.

LOOK FOR HOME GARDEN VARIETIES

Other things to consider in selecting seeds include growth habit. Peas and most species of beans are offered in both "bush" and "pole" varieties. The bush varieties make compact growth. In my experience they produce very well. Rows of bush varieties take little space and need no staking. Pole varieties need lots of space when grown in rows and must be staked. They also usually are a little slower to mature crops. But—if you want to grow some beans and have 4 square feet to do it in, plant a stake in the center and grow one of the climbers up around it. Or grow them up a strong trellis against the house.

Some vegetables are best (especially in regions with shorter growing seasons, as New England) set out as seedlings. Garden supply centers usually offer started seedlings in flats (tomatoes, cucumbers, bell, or sweet, peppers, hot peppers, cabbages, lettuce, broccoli, herbs, and many other food plants). If you have sunny windows you can start your own indoors in late winter and that's more fun. (See below.)

Seed packets give instructions on how deep to plant the seed and date for planting. Many have geographical charts in miniature to guide you in deciding the correct planting date for your area. The United States Department of Agriculture publishes a useful map of zones of plant hardiness. It shows the ranges of minimum temperatures for the whole country. It can be used to determine which varieties of plants will flourish in your garden.

BUYING FRUIT PLANTS

If you can, buy young orchard trees and bush fruit (strawberries and rhubarb) from local garden supply centers. Fruit plants (except melons) are perennials and must be able to withstand winter conditions in your area. Local sources generally are careful to sell only species and varieties resistant to local winter temperatures.

For small gardens, the best choices are the dwarf orchard trees, and not all local garden centers carry these. Catalogs do offer them. In making a catalog selection, carefully read the information given to make sure the producer guarantees the plant will survive in your climate.

For recommendations on varieties and species see the Dictionary of Plants, Section III.

POLLINATION

Some fruits require cross-pollination to set fruit. Among them are many varieties of apples and pears. Most, but not all, peach and nectarine varieties are self-pollinating. Plums require cross-pollination. Sour cherries pollinate themselves, but the big dark cherries do not. (See the table of Fruit Yields.)

Varieties requiring cross-pollination must be planted close to a variety that can pollinate it. The local Agricultural Extension Service can recommend cross-pollinating pairs suitable for your area in the species or varieties you wish to plant.

SOWING SEEDS

Seeds are generally sown in "drills," "broadcast" (see illustration) or in "hills" (see illustration). The Dictionary of Plants recommends a method for each entry.

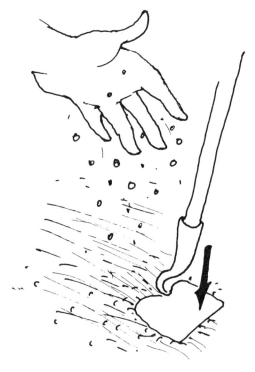

Broadcast sowing; tamp seed firmly into soil.

The sequence for planting your vegetable garden is illustrated here. You first improve the soil, as described in the preceding chapter, correcting composition or structure, to make a good garden loam. Then you add a general fertilizer and correct pH imbalances, if any. This can be done—and ideally is done—in the fall so that the garden is ready to plant as soon as the heavy winter moisture has gone, or in early spring.

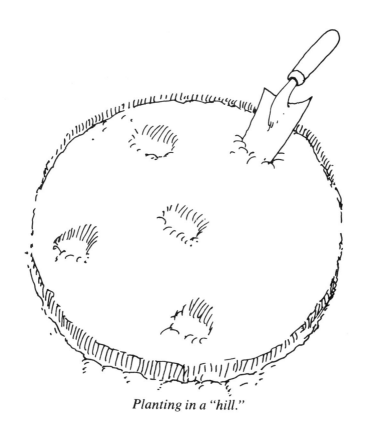

Planting in a "hill."

The steps that follow are illustrated. Dig the prepared soil to a depth of 2 inches and rake it smooth. With the string pegged in place use the pointed or square hoe to create a shallow trench under the string. Then plant the seeds in the trench, cover gently with soil, and water well.

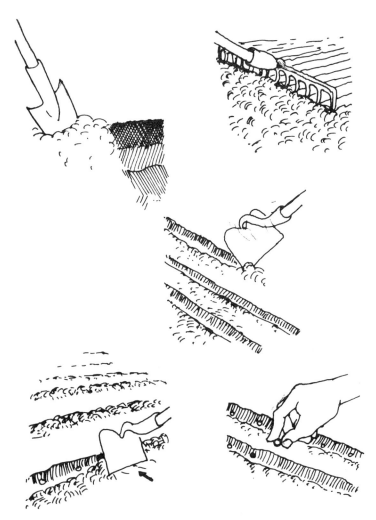

Dig the vegetable bed. Rake it smooth. Make drills or furrows with a hoe. Plant seeds. Cover the seeds with soil; tamp firmly.

To mark and identify the row, spear the seed packet on a sharp sturdy twig and plant it at the end of the row.

Seed sown by broadcasting are firmed gently into the soil after planting and then watered lightly. Radishes are one plant I sow by broadcasting. There aren't many.

Hill planting simply means that seeds are sown in groups, as illustrated, instead of in rows, or drills.

PLANTING FRUIT TREES

Fruit trees require good garden loam (what doesn't?) with pH on the acid side, full sun, and good drainage. Avoid planting in low areas where frosts settle in early fall and late spring, and look for sheltered spots where they won't get the dessicating sweep of north winds.

The hole for a fruit tree should be big enough to hold the root comfortably and deep enough to set the tree at the level at which it grew in the nursery. Some of the dwarfed fruit stock has special depth requirements and the instructions covering these are provided with the plant.

Fruit plants from local centers are usually sold "balled-and-burlapped," that is, the root is in a ball of soil, and the whole is wrapped in burlap or plastic.

Some mail order producers ship stock in a state called "bare-root"—that is, they ship still-dormant plants whose roots have been stripped of soil to make the shipment lighter. Bare-root plants usually transplant well if they are set into the ground before their buds begin to sprout. Soak bare-root plants well before planting.

Don't set stock to be planted in the burning sunlight while you dig the planting hole. Keep plants shaded, out of the wind, and in a cool spot if you can. Set balled-and-burlapped plants into their planting holes in the burlap covers. Shovel soil into the hole until the hole is about ⅔ full, then straighten the tree, firm the soil well with your feet, and check again to make sure the tree is straight. Fill the planting hole with water and after it has drained out, fill the hole to the crown with soil. (The crown is the point where the tree trunk meets the roots.) Water again thoroughly, then make a saucer of soil around the tree so that water won't run off when it rains.

Trees shipped bare-root are planted on a mound hilled at the bottom of the planting hole. Make a firm mound of soil meant to bring the crown of the tree to just below soil level and carefully and gently spread the tree roots over the mound. Make sure the tree is straight, then proceed to fill and water as described for balled-and-burlapped trees.

Most standard (regular) size and some dwarf and semi-dwarf fruit trees require pruning after planting, and the illustration gives a notion of how severe the pruning should be.

Pruning newly planted orchard fruits.

The pruning is meant to create a good shape for the tree, and also to lessen strain on the root system of the plant which may have been severely cut back or damaged during transplanting or shipment.

PLANTING BRAMBLE FRUITS

Blackberries and raspberries and other berries listed in the Dictionary of Plants are called bramble fruits and grow as low, often thorny, shrubs. They are sold, as are the orchard fruits, by local centers and through catalogs. Set the plants 12 inches apart in trenches of a depth that brings the crowns of the plants to the level they grew at in the nursery, and about 6 feet apart. Prepare the soil for the planting as you would garden soil.

Many gardeners stake raspberries to produce better yields. Pruning to improve yield is described by growers when it will help. Pruning of bramble fruits after planting is a common practice. At planting time, prune all branches back to 6 to 8 inches from the ground. Remove blossoms the first year.

Specific information for each fruit species appears in the Dictionary of Food Plants, Section III. Fruits grown in the open garden, such as strawberries, are discussed in Chapters Five, Six and Seven; grapes are discussed in Chapter Nine.

SEEDLINGS

In a sunny window or under grow lights, using peat or plastic flats (shallow planters) or pots and potting soil, you can start your own crop of seedlings for transplanting outdoors. One

Light garden with trays of seedlings growing indoors.

71

advantage to starting your own is that you then can be sure that the variety you prefer is available as a seedling. And starting your own is far less costly than buying started plants.

Most seeds should be started 4 to 8 weeks before the date for setting out in the open garden: 4 weeks for fast-growing plants, and 8 weeks for slow growers. A check of the Days To Maturity table will make clear what fast growers and slow growers are.

EQUIPMENT AND SOIL

Flats and peat pots are offered by catalogs and by local supply centers. You can substitute the big glass refrigerator trays, baking tins, or anything large that won't be harmed by

Peat pots—pressed peat moss—are ideal for starting seedlings since both pot and its seedling can go into the earth when it is time to transplant. Peat containers are essential for success when growing the vegetable that won't transplant well—notably cucumbers, melons, squashes, and gourds.

soil and has a 3- to 4-inch depth. You can use regular plastic or clay pots, too, or empty cans. Peat containers are desirable because you can plant container and all.

Bagged potting soil for indoor plants is suitable for starting seedlings. Or dig up garden soil, mix it with ⅓ sand and ⅓ fine peat moss or vermiculite, and use that. Do not fertilize the soil, or the plants will grow leggy.

One method for starting seedlings is to fill flats or peat pots almost to the rim with soil, and cover with 1 inch sphagnum moss. Sow the seed in the sphagnum moss, water gently, cover with plastic or glass to preserve moisture, and place in a warm, sunny room to germinate. But not on a window ledge.

Another method is to plant directly on the soil, without sphagnum. This method is illustrated here, in an herb-planting sequence.

Herb planting in individualized peat moss containers or pressed cardboard flats begins with the watering of the planting medium. (Photo by J. F. Michajluk.)

When the seedlings are up, move the containers to a sunny window ledge, and remove the covering.

If the plants yellow, let them dry out, then water them with a half-strength solution of ammonium nitrate.

Plant the seeds and cover with a fine scattering of soil; mark the pans so you will know which is which when it is time to move the seedlings to the open garden. (Photo by J. F. Michajluk.)

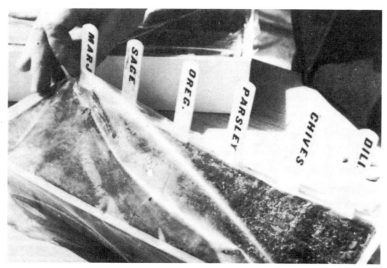

Cover the flat with plastic; it keeps the soil evenly moist and encourages quick germination of the seedlings. In the case of herbs, this is particularly important, as many herbs are slow to germinate. (Photo by J. F. Michajluk.)

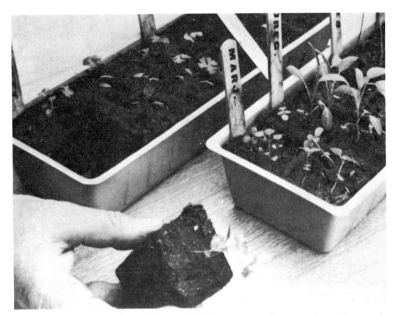

When plants are 3 inches tall, thin away the weakest in each square or pot leaving a single plant to grow. When the weather is right, transplant to the open garden. (Photo by J. F. Michajluk.)

As the seedlings grow, thin them frequently to avoid crowding. You can transplant most seedlings (but not cucumbers or squashes) into other containers. I use tweezers to transplant really small seedlings. Make sure before you take the time to transplant the thinnings, that you'll have room for them in your garden.

TRANSPLANT SEEDLINGS TO GARDEN

Seedlings living in lush comfort indoors require some hardening before they can be set out into the open garden. A week before planting time, allow the soil to dry out. The plants should not start to wilt. Set the flats outdoors in a spot with a little sun, and each day, move them into a sunnier location. If the night temperature threatens to drop severely, bring them indoors for the night. If you don't have time to harden them before planting, cover them for their first few days outdoors. Big brown supermarket bags make excellent temporary shelters.

To transplant the seedlings use a trowel to make holes larger than the plant to be set into them, and deep enough to bring the surface of the seedling earth ball to about ½ inch below ground level. Mix starter solution according to the packet directions in a big plastic pail, and pour ½ cup of this into each hole before planting. Before the water seeps away, set the plant into the hole. When the hole has drained, fill it loosely with earth, then firm the plant into its hole.

To cut apart seedlings growing in flats, use a sharp knife. Many tear apart easily, but you usually do more damage by pulling at the roots than you do with a sharp clean cut.

Part III

DICTIONARY OF FOOD PLANTS

Chapter Five

PLANT THESE IN EARLY SPRING

There are three main planting dates for vegetables and fruits—early spring, mid-spring, and late spring. These dates are keyed by the growth habits of the plants themselves. There are vegetables that grow well in cool weather. These are planted in earliest spring, or early-to-mid spring, and mature before real summer sets in. Second crops of these can be planted when the weather cools off toward the end of summer. Cabbage is one example of this type of vegetable.

Other crops grow best when planted in mid-spring. These won't withstand really cool weather or light frosts. Among these are beans and tomatoes.

And there are a few crops that shouldn't be planted until the temperature stays above 70 degrees. These are the late spring starters and among them are melons and eggplant.

The Dictionary of Food Plants that follows has been divided into seasonal planting chapters geared to these three main planting periods. The calendar dates representing each period depends on the climate of the region the plant is to grow in.

"AS SOON AS THE GROUND CAN BE WORKED"

In the coolest parts of Vermont, the calendar date on which the ground can be worked is rarely late March, sometimes early April, most often mid-to-late April. It depends on the year. It is the moment when the snow has gone and the ground, heavy and wet with winter, has dried enough so that a handful of soil squeezed into a ball in your hand crumbles readily under slight pressure from your thumb. There may still be some late frosts in valley pockets, but the very earliest of the cool weather crops—peas, lettuce, onion—are rarely affected by them.

Moving southward, "as soon as the ground can be worked" happens earlier in the calendar year so that in northern Florida you can expect to have crops harvested before they are planted in Vermont.

SOME EXCEPTIONS TO THE EARLY SPRING PLANTING RULE

There are some exceptions to the early spring planting rule. Peas can be planted before the ground can be worked (and the entry on peas tells how) but only if the bed has been dug in fall and is ready to plant as soon as the snow melts.

The reason we don't work the soil before it passes the snowball test described above is that to turn over and dig soaked, frozen soil compacts it and makes it lumpy, bumpy, and difficult for plant roots to grow in.

Before you start to plant, dig up soil prepared as described in Chapter Four, rake it smooth, then mark the planting row with pegged string so that it will be straight.

In laying out the garden, set the rows at an angle that allows all the plants to catch day-long sunlight, if possible. Romaine lettuce, pumpkins, and tomatoes can stand a little less than full sunlight, so plant these in any spot receiving noon shading from nearby trees or shrubs. Don't put a row of tall lush leaves between the sun and a row of cucumber vines.

GETTING READY TO PLANT

Plan to plant only as much as you can comfortably handle at any given session. Don't spoil your pleasure in gardening by trying to get it all in in an hour. Take the planting plan with you to the garden along with a hose set up so you can water well after planting, the hoe for marking rows, the peg and string for keeping rows straight, and use the rake or the back of the hoe to fill in the trenches after the seeds are in.

GETTING A HEAD START

Since lots of seeds intended for early spring planting can be started indoors and set out when the ground is ready, you should be planting seeds in flats 1 to 2 months before you expect to set them out.

A word of warning—if you become very ambitious in the starting of seedlings, your house will be flooded with too many flats holding too many seedlings for comfort. It takes two or three flats to contain a small package of seeds as started seedlings—so think through how many you really want to start indoors and how much space there is for them in sunny windows before you begin. You can start dozens of flats indoors under grow lights, of course. Or, you can buy lots of plants as started seedlings in garden supply centers.

KEY TO THE LEGEND AT THE TOP OF EACH ENTRY

Sow (numbers) seeds per foot is a general indication of about the right number of seeds per foot. It can be followed more or less exactly—you don't have to count out the number of seeds per foot. When dropping seed into the bed the main point is to keep them some inches apart so the seedlings won't crowd each other as they grow.

Germinates in (number) days is the length of time it takes before the seedlings show a green fuzz just above the surface of the soil. This is helpful information since it will keep you from mistaking a crop of weeds for the plants you have sown. If you sow the seed in a straight row, the alignment of the baby plants will also help you to know whether what you see is a plant or a lush crop of baby weeds.

Transplant in (number) days or weeks suggests when to start seeds indoors.

Plants mature in (number) days or weeks tells when you can expect to harvest this crop if it is set out as a "plant," a started seedling, and is helpful in the planning of a continuous round of crops. If all the plants in your garden are going to be ready for harvest at the same time, your planting plan is a failure. The planting plan should be worked out in such a way that you have some salad makings all season long and one or two vegetables maturing each week throughout the season.

Seeds mature in (number) days or weeks tells how long it will take this crop to reach harvest time if it is set out as seed rather than as started seedlings.

ASPARAGUS

Sow 2- or 3-year-old roots
Matures the second and third year

SMALL GARDEN NOTES: Asparagus is a perennial plant set out in the garden as a root. Asparagus spears appear above the ground in early spring, and as the season progresses, those not picked for eating grow into tall feathery ferns florists give away with bouquets. Throughout the summer months they are beautiful as a backdrop to lower-growing flowers—and so they fit well anywhere in the small garden. An area 10-feet square will supply all a family of three can use, once the plants are established. The plants are generally sold by the dozen, and two dozen mature plants will provide a lot of asparagus. Asparagus is most successful in areas where roots freeze in winter.

VARIETIES TO CONSIDER: Mary Washington and Waltham Washington are two improved strains resistant to diseases that attack asparagus. In buying roots, consider the 2-year roots rather than the 3-year-old roots offered for more money. You'll have to wait until the second year for a crop in either case, and won't have a flourishing asparagus bed until the third year the plants are in, however mature the roots planted were to start with.

PLANTING SCHEDULE. Set out the roots in early spring as soon as the ground can be worked.

PLANTING: Since asparagus is a perennial, prepare the bed well. A rich soil supplied with rotted manure, compost, or peat moss and fertilizer produces a lush crop. Dig holes or trenches 2 to 4 feet apart, 8 to 10 inches deep, 12 inches wide, and mix

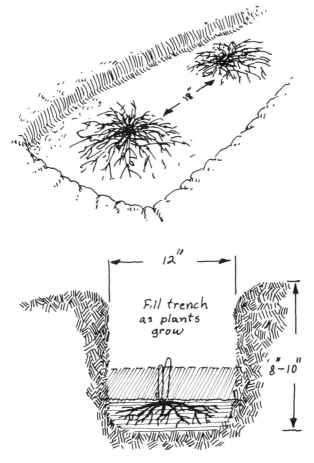

Planting asparagus roots.

83

the soil from the trenches with one-third sharp sand, if available. Work the soil in the floor of the trench with 1 inch of manure, compost, or dried cow manure, or 1 inch peat and fertilizer at the rate recommended on the package. On the floor of the trench, make a hump of soil, and over this spread the asparagus roots. Roots should be 18 inches apart. Cover the roots with 2 inches of soil, and as the spears grow, fill in the trench over them, until it is level with the ground.

CULTURE: Each spring, early, work a handful of compost or manure or 1 tablespoon of complete fertilizer into the soil around each plant. Three or so weeks later, just before spear growth starts, work ½ ounce of nitrate of soda in around each plant. After the harvest is over, rake ½ pound of nitrate of soda into the soil for each 20 plants. Keep the soil around the plants well mulched, or cultivate to keep weeds down. Maturing beds throw seedlings every year. Transplant these in early spring to start a new row, or place them at the back of flower borders or in among deciduous shrubs. In early fall, cut away and burn all the tops.

HARVESTING: The harvest season for this early crop is from the time the spears start to appear until the plants slow production of the spears—4 to 6 weeks later, depending on the season. Keep all spears cut during the cutting season, but once growth slows, pick no more—let all the new spears grow into plants. Keep spears cut as they reach 6 to 8 inches in height. To cut, slide a sharp knife just under the surface of the soil, and slice through the spear at an angle.

BEETS

Sow 10–15 seeds per foot
Germinates in 7–10 days
Don't plan to transplant
Matures in 45–80 days

SMALL GARDEN NOTES: Beets grow well in soil 10 to 12 inches deep in any type of container. However, since their flavor is best when they are tiny, and it takes three to four small beets to make one serving, they are not particularly suited to small container gardens. For beets to be a really practical crop, the garden should have 10 to 25 feet of row space.

VARIETIES TO CONSIDER: Early Wonder (52 days to maturity) or Detroit Dark Red (60 days) are good standard varieties. Lutz Green Leaf (80 days) is a good one to plant for early fall harvest and winter keeping. Golden and white varieties are interesting new beets for the gardener who likes surprises.

PLANTING SCHEDULE: Make successive sowings at three-week intervals from early spring on in order to have a continuous crop. When sowing beets in midsummer heat, cover the row with a thin layer of mulch and keep it damp until the seeds are up.

PLANTING: Beets have small, lumpy seeds which sometimes are stuck together in twos and threes. They resent strongly acid soils. The soil in which they are most successful is a very

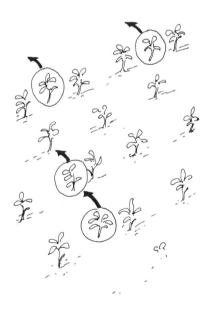

Thinning seedlings.

fertile loam with lots of humus, worked to a depth of 10 to 12 inches. If your beets come up fibrous instead of fine in texture, the loam is too sandy. Make a drill 1 inch deep, in the center of a 12-inch row. Cover the seeds with ½ inch of soil, and firm the soil with the back of the hoe. Water well. Mulch the row on either side of the planting furrow.

CULTURE: When the red-veined green leaves thicken and begin to crowd the drill, gently pull up enough so the remaining plants stand 2 to 3 inches apart. These "thinnings" make excellent "spinach" greens. (Wash them very well before cooking.) If you haven't mulched, cultivate the soil around the beets with the hoe to keep weeds down. If the row is mulched, pull the mulch up around the remaining plants to keep weeds away until harvest time.

HARVESTING: You can harvest second and third crops of beet leaves as long as the beets are in the row. Pick one or two tender young leaves from each plant until you have enough for a meal. Do not strip any one plant of too many leaves at one time. The beet roots are ready for harvest when they are 3 inches around. You can let them remain in the soil for several weeks after they grow to 3 inches, but the smaller beets are the finest. The greens from the beets harvested can also be cooked for greens. Discard any discolored, chewed, or visibly tough leaves. When picking beets for dinner, go over the row and pull out the largest. Those remaining will grow and be ready for the next mess of beets you pull. To get the roots up, grasp the stems where they join the base and pull gently. If this doesn't work, loosen the soil with a trowel, then pull the beet up.

BROCCOLI

Sow 10–15 seeds per foot
Germinates in 3–10 days
Transplant in 5–7 weeks
Plant matures in 56–60 days
Seed matures in 80–100 days

SMALL GARDEN NOTES: Broccoli grows 2 to 3 feet tall so

if it is going into a flower border, set it at the back. Each plant requires 1½ to 2 feet of space all around. Each plant yields one large broccoli head and some smaller side heads after the main head has been cut so consider whether this is a plant that will give a large enough harvest for the space it will require. Unless you have a 10 to 25 feet of row space to give to broccoli, you may not consider it a good candidate.

VARIETIES TO CONSIDER: Heading broccoli is difficult to grow, so choose the varieties called "sprouting broccoli." Green Comet, Calabrese, and De Cicco are good choices.

PLANTING SCHEDULE: Plants started indoors 5 to 6 weeks before the ground is ready for planting begin to yield sprouts 50 to 60 days after they are set in the open ground. Start seedlings indoors, for a late fall harvest, 5 weeks before midsummer.

PLANTING: In cool climates, start broccoli seeds indoors 5 to 6 weeks before the ground will be ready for planting, and set the seedlings out as soon as the ground is ready. If you have 12 to 15 weeks of cool growing weather ahead by the time the ground can be worked, then sow seed outdoors in drills, 1 inch deep with 20 to 24 inches between each row. Cover the seeds with ½ inch of soil, tamp firm. If you are setting out seedlings, plant 18 inches apart in the row and ½ inch below their previous planting level. Water well. Mulch on either side of the seeds.

CULTURE: When the plants are 3 inches tall, thin them so they stand 18 inches apart in the row. The seedlings can be transplanted if you have space. If you haven't mulched, cultivate with a hoe to keep weeds down until the plants are growing well. If the row is mulched, pull the mulch up around the thinned seedlings, and keep it thick enough to eliminate the possibility of weeds. Just before the broccoli matures—when it is a small fat head of buds—work a tablespoon of 4-8-4 (or your own balanced fertilizer) into the soil around each plant to encourage the plants to form a second crop.

HARVESTING: Cut the sprouts cleanly from the plants, 6 inches below the florets; other sprouts will develop in the axils of the leaves. Harvest before the buds begin to break open— the flavor is best then.

NOTE: Broccoli is a member of the *brassica* group of vegetables, which includes cabbage, cauliflower, and Brussels
sprouts. Don't plant a *brassica* where another *brassica* was the
crop the year before. Pull the plant and remove to the compost
pile as soon as it has been harvested.

BRUSSELS SPROUTS

Sow 10–15 seeds per foot
Germinates in 3–10 days
Transplant in 4–6 weeks
Plant matures in 60–70 days
Seed matures in 95 days

SMALL GARDEN NOTES: A single Brussels sprouts plant
yields quite a few of these tiny cabbages, and it's rather fun
to see how many sprouts develop in the axils of the leaves. So,
even if your space is limited to room for half a dozen, I think
they are worth considering for the very small garden. The
plants grow to be very tall, however, so choose their setting
carefully. They will live outdoors over winter in the milder
sections, and may be grown as a winter crop in the South.

VARIETIES TO CONSIDER: Jade Cross is a good choice—
it's a hybrid offered by most suppliers.

PLANTING SCHEDULE: Plan on one crop, set out as a
seedling in early spring for early fall harvest.

PLANTING AND CULTURE: The planting instructions for
Brussels sprouts are similar to those for broccoli. Scratch a
tablespoon of 4-8-4 in around each plant when the first Brussels
sprouts show as tiny buds in the leaf axils to encourage long
season harvest.

HARVESTING: As the heads swell and begin to crowd the
leaves, break off the leaf below each. Sprouts have the finest
flavor when they are about 1½ inches in diameter. Pick them
just before using. If frost threatens before the sprout harvest is
complete, dig up the plants and set them close together with

their roots in a heap of damp sand or soil in a cool place—a cellar or a cold frame. The sprouts will keep well for several more weeks of harvesting.

The same cautions described in the note under Broccoli apply to Brussels sprouts.

CABBAGE

Sow 8–10 seeds per foot
Germinates in 4–10 days
Transplant in 5–7 weeks
Matures in 40–90 days

SMALL GARDEN NOTES: Two or three dozen cabbages are as much as the average family will want. Each plant produces one head.

VARIETIES TO CONSIDER: There are two kinds of cabbage for the home garden: the loose-headed leafy green cabbage of early spring, and the big, tightly-closed heavy heads harvested in fall and winter. In the North, plant spring cabbage for an early crop, late cabbage for winter storing. Savoy cabbage with its crinkled leaves is attractive in beds of flowers, so this is a variety to chose for a mixed border. Red cabbage is attractive, too. All except Chinese cabbage (also called Wong Bok or celery cabbage) can be started indoors to provide seedlings for outdoor planting. Chinese is a good choice for the gourmet garden—it is good in salads or cooked, and wonderful for use with Oriental dishes. It is best as an autumn crop in the northern states and as a winter crop in the South. Earliana, Early Jersey Wakefield, and Golden Acre are standard heading cabbages for the early-season planting. Copenhagen Market, Globe, and Stonehead are midseason choices. Flat Dutch and Danish Ballhead are recommended for late planting and winter growing. Where cabbage yellows are a problem, select resistant varieties— Stonehead, early season; Marron Market and Globe for midseason; Wisconsin Hollander for late crops. A handsome green and gold Savory variety is Savoy King (90 days to maturity).

Red Acre (75 days to maturity) is a good red. Ruby Ball is an early red that matures in 68 days. Little Leaguer cabbage is a Burpee midget that matures in 60 days, and is the right choice for cabbage to be grown in a very small or container garden—the mature heads are about 4 inches around and excellent in flavor.

PLANTING SCHEDULE: In the far South grow cabbage in all seasons except summer. As far north as Washington, D.C., set out cabbage in fall for spring harvest. In the North, try for one early spring crop and one late fall crop.

PLANTING: See Broccoli. Cabbages require a very fertile soil. Add side dressings of nitrate of soda, sulfate of ammonia, or another quickly available nitrogen fertilizer at intervals of 3 weeks—about ⅓ ounce for each plant.

HARVESTING: As cabbage heads are maturing, watch them closely—left too long in the garden, they will split. If you've had enough cabbage for the time being, pull the plants hard enough to break the roots loose, and leave them standing in the garden. Unlike broccoli, cabbage plants produce only one harvest, a single head.

The cautions found in the note under Broccoli also apply to cabbage.

CARROTS

Sow 15–20 seeds per foot
Germinates in 10–17 days
Don't plan to transplant
Plant matures in 65–75 days
Seed matures in 80–100 days

SMALL GARDEN NOTES: You can grow a fine crop of delicious baby carrots in a stepped garden, a container garden, or in a sunny corner of the landscape, however small. Plant them in round patches instead of drills (rows); they'll grow beautifully as long as the instructions below are followed—and the delicate ferny tops, 6 to 10 inches tall, make them decorative. A good choice for the small garden.

VARIETIES TO CONSIDER: Oxheart and Short 'n Sweet varieties are especially suited to the shallow soils of container gardens and Oxheart is more successful in heavy soils than many other varieties. Tiny Sweet is a delicious miniature for gourmets. Chantenay, Nantes, and Imperator are standard choices.

PLANTING SCHEDULE: Carrots can be planted in the fall in the South, and from earliest spring through summer in the North. Carrots are hardy and should be one of the first sowing scheduled. Succession plantings at 3 week intervals will produce a continuous crop.

PLANTING: Carrots are finicky about the loam they grow in. In rocky ground, they come out knobby little lumps and in soil that is too sandy, they become fibrous. To have straight, long, handsome carrots, you require fine, deeply worked loam. Make a furrow ½ inch deep and 12 inches wide, and broadcast the carrot seed evenly over the bed. Carrot seeds are very fine. Mixed with coffee grounds they are easier to spread evenly. I often plant quick-to-sprout radish seeds with carrot seeds to discourage weeds and keep the row producing while waiting for the carrots. Cover with ¼ inch fine soil, tamp, and water well but lightly. Mulch on either side of the row.

CULTURE: Because carrots are very slow to germinate, the drills often become infested with crabgrass before the seedlings come up. Weeding then becomes a problem, because as you pull the vigorous crabgrass seedlings, the baby carrots come up with them. Try to keep the bed weeded, if necessary by hand, until the carrots are sprouted and growing. "Don't plant carrots where crabgrass went to seed last year" is one of my favorite cautions for those who hate weeding. Thin the seedlings when the carrot ferns begin to crowd each other. Then weed the bed painstakingly and mulch as closely as you can to the seedlings.

HARVESTING: When you can see the green-to-orange tops of the maturing carrots through the soil, they are generally ready to harvest. Pull the larger ones as you spot them, thinning the row, and leaving more space for the remaining carrots to mature. The sweetest flavor is in half-grown carrots.

CAULIFLOWER

Sow 8–10 seeds per foot
Germinates in 4–10 days
Transplant in 5–7 weeks
Plants mature in 50–60 days
Seeds mature in 80–90 days

SMALL GARDEN NOTES: Cauliflower is a tall plant that produces a single head—so the number of plants you set out is the number of heads you will harvest. One to two dozen is plenty for the average family. For an ornamental garden, try the purple cauliflowers. The heads turn a glorious color, smashing as a centerpiece (though green once cooked) and the flavor is excellent.

VARIETIES TO CONSIDER: Early Snowball produces small to medium heads in about 60 days and is a good choice for spring harvesting. Snow King Hybrid (50 days) is extremely early and similar in type. Purple Head (80–85 days to maturity) tastes a little like broccoli and needs no blanching.

PLANTING SCHEDULE: Hardy, though not as hardy as cabbage, cauliflower won't head in warm weather. In the South, plant it in fall, winter, and early spring. In the North, plant cauliflower when the frosts are over in spring, and again in August so it will be reaching the heading stage after the weather has cooled. Start seedlings indoors, 5–7 weeks before planting time, and set out when there are 50–60 days of growing weather before either real heat or fall frosts are due.

PLANTING: See Broccoli

CULTURE: See Broccoli

HARVESTING: Those big, beautifully creamy heads of cauliflower sold in specialty shops have generally been blanched. Heads left to mature uncovered develop a lilac or green tinge. To blanch your crop, cover the heads with newspaper or paper bags (unsealed to allow air circulation) or tie the big leaves up over each head with raffia or a rag 2 or 3 weeks before the head is ready to harvest. To harvest, just cut the head where it meets the main stem.
See Note under Broccoli.

CHARD

Sow 6–10 seed per foot
Germinates in 7–10 days
Don't plan to transplant
Matures in 55–60 days

SMALL GARDEN NOTES: Swiss chard looks like rhubarb and is a type of beet, developed for its top instead of its roots. It will grow where spinach presents problems, and the leafy part of the plant makes excellent greens for cooking. The leaves can be harvested from the time the plant begins to mature until frosts wilt it, so it is a long-season crop. Six to 10 plants are sufficient to supply an average family. They look well tucked in among the medium-height flowers in an ornamental border. The stalks aren't cooked with the greens, but are treated by many gourmets like asparagus spears, and can also be stuffed and braised, or creamed.

VARIETIES TO CONSIDER: Fordhook Giant has richly green leaves and pearly white stalks. It looks great in the ornamental garden and the greens are exceptionally tender. Rhubarb chard has crimson stalks and is more striking in appearance.

PLANTING SCHEDULE: Only one planting is necessary— the plants will keep producing throughout the summer until frosts.

PLANTING: Avoid excessively acid soil for chard. Sow the seeds in drills 2 inches deep, in rows 18 inches apart and cover with ¼ inch of fine soil. The drill will fill with soil as the plants mature. Tamp lightly, water, mulch.

CULTURE: When the plants are 3 inches tall, pull the weakest seedlings leaving the remaining plants 4 inches apart. When the plants are twice as tall, thin the plants to 6 inches apart. The thinnings thoroughly washed are delicious braised. In mid-season, when they are halfway mature, work a handful of 4-8-4, or your own complete fertilizer, in around each plant to encourage lush production all season long.

HARVESTING: Pick the outer leaves by giving them a sharp twist. Don't pick too many from any one plant at one time.

CHICORY

Sow 8–10 seeds per foot
Germinates in 5–12 days
Don't plan to transplant
Matures in 112 days

SMALL GARDEN NOTES: Chicory is a salad green offered by specialty shops and in some supermarkets. It is a gourmet salad green, a good choice for gardeners who like sharp flavors. Chicory is related to endive and escarole in flavor. It is a good companion planting for tall-standing long-season crops, such as corn. The curly low-growing leaves are attractive and can be tucked into flower borders as a leafy accent. Grow it in containers, stepped gardens, even in a window box.

SOME VARIETIES TO CONSIDER: Witloaf, or French endive, is the name under which chicory seed is offered in many catalogs.

PLANTING SCHEDULE: One sowing after frosts are completely gone is a good investment of space.

PLANTING: Sow the seeds, broadcast thinly over well-dug, smoothly raked companion planting beds or rows, rake them into the soil lightly, and tamp. Or, sow the seeds 4 inches apart over furrows 4 inches wide and ½ inch deep. Cover with ¼ inch fine soil, tamp, water well, and mulch sides of the row.

CULTURE: As the seedlings grow, pull these at the outer edges to make room for the remaining plants. With the root removed and the leaves thoroughly washed, the thinnings make excellent salads.

HARVESTING: Chicory that has dark leaves and golden white inner hearts have been blanched. When the heads are maturing, tie the outer leaves together over the center with a soft rag or raffia to keep the light from the developing inner section. If the plants are standing in a straight row, you can place a light plank over the center of the heads and achieve the same result with less effort. To harvest, cut the head from the root at the base.

CRESS

Sow 6–8 seeds per foot
Germinates in 4–10 days
Don't plan to transplant
Matures in 20 days

SMALL GARDEN NOTES: Cress—often called garden cress
—is a good choice for the devotee of watercress who doesn't
happen to have a stream in which to grow it. Cress produces a
long stem with fine green leaves that have a peppery flavor.
One of its great virtues is the fact that it grows easily in a
window box as in the open garden, and is up and out of the
ground 3 to 4 weeks after sowing. It will also grow indoors,
in a cool, sunny, airy spot. It is a good companion planting
for slow-to-germinate species, like carrots, and a good preceding crop for many of the plants sown in mid- or late spring
(see Chapters Six and Seven).

VARIETIES TO CONSIDER: Not all suppliers offer seeds.
They sometimes are called Peppergrass (erroneously) and
sometimes Upland Cress. Curlycress is a variety to begin to
pick in about 10 days. Salad cress is a variety slow to bolt.

PLANTING SCHEDULE: Sow indoors any time, or outdoors
at any point, during the growing season. Because this crop
matures in just a few weeks, it is a good filler to occupy space
before or after a slower crop. For a steady season-long supply,
sow seed every 2 weeks.

PLANTING: See Lettuce. Space cress plants 12 inches apart,
with 24 inches between rows.

CULTURE: In 4 to 10 days skinny green stems will appear.
After they are well established, thin them to stand 12 inches
apart, and use the thinnings, well washed, in salads.

HARVESTING: Cut branches as needed.

DANDELIONS

Sow 6–10 seeds per foot
Germinates in 7–14 days
Don't plan to transplant
Matures the second season

SMALL GARDEN NOTES: Don't let the flowers go to seed—or your cultured planting will spawn the weeds in your, and neighboring, yards. The dandelions stubbornly reappearing season after season in your lawn make a natural crop, free for the picking, so think twice before you allot small garden space to this green. Dandelions are sweeter and more tender if you blanch them, whether wild or cultivated, by tying outer leaves together with a bit of wool a week or so before harvesting. The inner leaves (and flowers) will be pale and are delicious in salads and cooked as greens. Dandelions are one of nature's toughest constructions and will grow anywhere.

VARIETIES TO CONSIDER: Thick-leaved is a variety for gardens and matures in 95 days, or early the following season, depending on climate. The greens are used for boiling, as spinach.

PLANTING SCHEDULES: Seed planted this spring will produce mature plants by the end of the season, but this won't be good to eat. Since dandelions are perennials, next spring the crop will reappear, ready for harvesting in early spring.

PLANTING: See Lettuce, but space rows 18 inches apart, and thin plants to 4 inches apart.

CULTURE: If plants begin to look limp in midseason—don't panic. Add a handful of fertilizer to the row.

HARVESTING: Harvest in early spring, after blanching as described above.

JERUSALEM ARTICHOKE

Matures in 120 days

SMALL GARDEN NOTES: The Jerusalem artichoke, a starchless potato-like staple of the American Indians, is a perennial and grows as high as 12 feet tall and bears sunflower-yellow blooms. The tubers are dug and eaten in early fall. A good choice if you like the artichoke-like flavor and have space for a tall, flowering plant that doubles as a vegetable. Leave some of the stand to grow on; the tubers multiply rapidly and will provide next year's harvest.

VARIETIES TO CONSIDER: These plants are not offered by most catalogs—so keep your eyes open for specialty markets offering the roots.

PLANTING SCHEDULE: Plant in early spring in the North; early fall in the South.

PLANTING: If roots are not readily available buy fresh tubers at specialty food markets, divide them into sections each bearing two eyes, plant, and mulch well for next year's crop. Sow tuber pieces 3 inches deep, 18 inches apart, in hills or groups of six. Mulch around plantings.

CULTURE: When shoots are up, pull the mulch close to the stems, and keep well watered during the spring season. Fertilize with an all-purpose mixture when the plants are 24 inches tall.

HARVESTING: After top growth ceases in the early fall, dig the tubers, allow to dry on the hill for a day, and store in a cool place. To start a new patch for next year's harvest, leave a few tubers in the ground.

KALE

Sow 8–12 seeds per foot
Germinates in 3–10 days
Transplant in 4–6 weeks
Matures in 56–75 days

SMALL GARDEN NOTES: Kale is a vitamin-rich, leafy green for boiling as spinach, or using in salads. It is recommended for the small garden as a plant to sow in late summer for a fall crop of greens. The low-growing, spreading plants with thick, crinkly leaves are quite ornamental. Kale can be planted in containers, window boxes, and stepped gardens as well as in the open garden.

VARIETIES TO CONSIDER: Blue Curled and Dwarf Siberian are offered by most suppliers. Siberian is the hardier of the two and good for early fall crops in cool regions.

PLANTING SCHEDULES: Spring sowings may have trouble with weeds—and anyway, other boiling greens, notably spinach and beet tops, are available at this period, so consider kale for late summer and early fall planting. In latitudes as far north as northern Maryland and southern Pennsylvania, kale is hardy and lives over most winters with a little protection from hay or straw.

PLANTING: See Broccoli, but space rows 12 to 18 inches apart.

CULTURE: See Broccoli. When the plants are up and thriving, thin to stand 10 to 12 inches apart.

HARVESTING: Leaves left on the plant too long become dark green, chewy, and bitter, so when leaves turn bright green and crisp, immediately snap off as many outer leaves as needed. Freeze extras.

LEEKS

Sow 6–12 seeds per foot
Germinates in 7–12 days
Transplant in 10–12 weeks
Seed matures in 130 days

SMALL GARDEN NOTES: Leeks are like giant green onions with a mild flavor and are a staple in European soups and stews and in gourmet kitchens. They are not a particularly good choice when space is limited. They belong in the open garden and will occupy their row from early spring until early fall, when they are dug, dried, and stored for winter.

VARIETIES TO CONSIDER: Broad London, also known as American Flag, is offered by many suppliers.

PLANTING SCHEDULE: There's only one crop; sown in early spring, it matures a little over 4 months later.

PLANTING: In early spring sow the seeds 2 to 3 inches apart in drills ¼ inch deep, in rows 10 to 12 inches apart. Cover with a dusting of soil, and tamp.

CULTURE: When seedings are 2 inches high, thin every other plant and transplant thinnings to another row. When the leek tops are fat as pencils cut the tops back halfway, and replant seedlings in a 12-inch deep trench, spacing them 6 inches apart. As they grow, fill the trench, pushing soil against the bottom portions of the stalks. The process blanches the leeks. A short-cut method I find satisfactory is to thin the seedlings when they are 2 inches so they stand 6 inches apart. Gradually add soil to make a 3-inch high hill around the stalks.

HARVESTING: On a dry day, dig the leeks, pushing the spading fork down into the earth well below the roots; test the depth you are digging to make sure you are not slicing through the bottoms of the vegetables. Break the leeks away from the soil clumps, wash them thoroughly, let dry, then store in bunches in a cool place. Or, lift the clumps and store them in damp sand in a cellar, or store them in a cold frame.

LETTUCE

Sow 4–8 seeds per foot
Germinates in 4–10 days
Transplant in 3–5 weeks
Matures in 40–90 days

SMALL GARDEN NOTES: Lettuce should be included in the smallest of gardens for the sake of variety as well as economy. Pretty in any spot, Oak Leaf and Ruby lettuces, Bibb and Boston butterheads are a delightful change after winter's steady diet of Iceberg heads. Heading lettuce, of which Iceberg is one, is hard for the amateur gardener to grow successfully. It requires 85 to 90 days to mature and is not recommended. You can grow most other lettuces anywhere, in a window box or a planter, at the foot of a dwarf ornamental or fruit tree, in

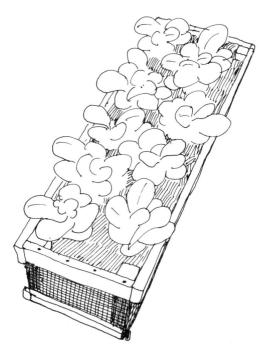

Lettuce growing in a window box.

among the petunias, wherever they are, among the herbs, or at the foot of tall growers like cabbage and corn in the open garden. You can grow lettuce as an edging for the open garden or a flower border, or primly in drills of its own.

VARIETIES TO CONSIDER: The lettuces divide more or less correctly into three types: butterheads such as Bibb, Boston, and Fordhook (which has heavier, fleshier leaves than Bibb or Boston); crisphead lettuces, which I call head lettuce (includes Iceberg); and loosehead or leaf lettuce (includes Oak Leaf and Ruby varieties). The butterheads, including Bibb and Boston which mature in 75 to 80 days, are well worth finding space for. The looseheading types mature in about 45 days. In early spring plant one sowing of butterheads and one or two of looseheads, if you want variety. Pick leaves from the looseheads as needed; the plant will go on producing until summer heat causes them to bolt. ("Bolted" lettuce throws up a central flowering stalk, at which point the leaves turn tough and bitter.) Pick the butterheads as they mature. When the weather gets really hot, almost all but the Cos or Romaine lettuces bolt. Distinctive from other lettuces, this type stands about 10 inches tall and has a naturally blanched, greenish white interior. It takes about 83 days to mature.

PLANTING SCHEDULE: For a season-long variety of lettuces, plant Oak Leaf and butterhead types in early spring for use through early summer, and plant Cos or Romaine at the same time for use through the hot months. Second sowings of Oak Leaf types may be made in midsummer for fall picking. Or, when space becomes available in beds or containers, plant Garden cress or chicory for fall salads. Lettuces are excellent subjects for interplanting, planting at the feet of tall, trim, longer-to-mature types of vegetables, such as cabbages, broccoli, corn, and at the feet of pole beans and other climbers, and in among the flowers in an ornamental border.

PLANTING: If you are going to intercrop, broadcast lettuce seeds thinly over prepared beds. Otherwise sow thickly in furrows 4 inches wide and ½ inch deep, with 12 inches between rows. Cover with ¼ inch of fine soil, tamp, water.

CULTURE: Thin as often as necessary to keep seedlings from crowding each other. Thinnings serve as tender additions to your salad bowl.

HARVESTING: Pick side leaves from loose lettuce types as needed. Cut heading varieties from the stalks close to the ground, and dig and discard roots.

NEW ZEALAND SPINACH

Sow 6–8 seeds per foot
Germinates in 6–14 days
Do not plan to transplant
Matures in 60–70 days

SMALL GARDEN NOTES: Half a dozen New Zealand spinach plants will provide boiling greens for a small family, and can be grown in among ornamentals in the flower border, or even in a bed with foundation plantings as long as the soil isn't exceptionally acid. Each plant should have 2 to 3 feet of space all around. New Zealand spinach tastes much like regular spinach, but unlike regular spinach, which is a spring crop finished by summer in most areas, the New Zealand plant thrives through the hot weather and tips can be harvested all season long until frosts wilt the plants.

VARIETIES TO CONSIDER: Catalogs offer seeds for this plant under the name New Zealand or Everlasting spinach. A plant with similar virtues, less well-known among gardeners perhaps, is Malabar spinach, a heat-resistant boiling green that grows as a vine and can be trained on a fence.

PLANTING SCHEDULE: Plant seeds in spring for summer picking. New Zealand spinach takes about 60 to 70 days to be ready and will produce for the rest of the growing season.

PLANTING: Place six to eight seeds every 12 inches in furrows ½ inch deep. Cover with ¼ inch of fine soil and tamp. Mulch around the plant.

CULTURE: Thin seedlings to stand 4 to 6 inches apart when seedlings are 3 inches high, and pull mulch up around the seedlings. When the plants are half-grown, scratch in a handful of nitrate of soda to provide nutrients for this long-season harvest.

HARVESTING: Do not harvest much from plants until they are flourishing. Then break off branch tips about 3 inches long, as needed. Don't remove too much from any individual plant at one time.

ONIONS

Sow sets 1–2 per foot
Sprout 10–12 days
Matures in 110 days

SMALL GARDEN NOTES: Onions can be grown from seed, but most often are grown from sets. Onion sets are the half-grown onions of seeds planted the season before. Sets are best for the home garden because they mature much more rapidly.

The uses of onions in the small garden are limited. Though fresh onions are nice, why waste space on a product not strikingly better than that sold at food counters? However, if you have a small garden and are interested in organic, or non-chemical ways of getting rid of pests, onions and members of the onion family, like leeks and multiplier or bunching onions, do have a place since they tend to keep pests away from plants nearby. Many organic gardeners report success in offsetting Japanese beetles when onions were planted around the roses. Onions worth giving space to for flavor and for economy are the big, sweet Bermuda or Spanish onions which are very costly in stores and wonderfully mild when just plucked from the garden. These should be set out as started seedlings—a green plant as opposed to the dried, tiny onion which is called an onion set—in early spring, to allow time for the onion to grow to maximum size.

VARIETIES TO CONSIDER: Yellow Bermuda, Granex, and White Granex, large, very mild, flat onions, are grown for spring harvest in the South. Sweet Spanish and the hybrids Golden Beauty, Fiesta, Bronze Perfection, El Capitan are large onions with a mild flavor, grown in the central latitudes. In the cooler regions, Southport White Globe, Yellow Globe, Early Yellow Globe, and some hybrids are good choices. Potato (multiplier) and Top (tree) onions are offered by some catalogs and are planted in the fall for spring use. Some catalogs offer seedlings.

PLANTING SCHEDULE: In the South, fall plantings of seeds produce spring crops. In cooler regions, plant sets in earliest spring for summer harvests; seedlings are planted in the spring for summer harvests.

PLANTING: Fertilizer is the key to onion growing. Add one pound of 4-8-4, or an equivalent product, and extra humus to every 20 feet of row. After the last frost, plant onion sets with pointed tips up in 1-inch-deep holes, 8 inches apart, and cover with ½ inch of soil.

If you want to start from scratch, sow seeds in furrows ½ inch deep with ¼ inch of soil and tamp well because night crawlers tend to dislodge seeds. If planting onion seedlings, set in furrow 3 inches deep, cover with 2½ inches soil, tamp. Mulch the row and water well.

CULTURE: Once plants are scallion size, pick often, until

smaller variety plants are 5 inches apart and larger varieties are 8 inches apart.

HARVESTING: When flowers appear among the onion leaves, bend the stalks in half, and plan to harvest in about 10 days later. Pull up onions by roots if the soil is loose. If you have difficulty, use a spading fork. Strew the onions on the garden soil to cure until the tops dry out, or rain threatens. Drying can be finished in a sunny window, if necessary. When dry, rub off the soil, braid the stems into bunches 18 inches long. They will keep in a dry cool place until spring, when they tend to sprout. Perennial bunching onions can be left in the garden through the winter and picked as needed. All onion seedlings may be pulled and used as green onions at any point in their early growth.

PARSNIPS

Sow 8–12 seeds per foot
Germinates in 15–25 days
Do not plant to transplant
Matures in 95–150 days

SMALL GARDEN NOTES: The parsnip is a root vegetable, and to my mind one of the best. However, parsnips require fairly deep soil and the sometime straggly leaves don't make them particularly suited to container gardening or the flower border. However, do consider them for summer planting for a late-fall/early-winter harvest if you have space in a row in the garden at the end of the summer.

VARIETIES TO CONSIDER: All American (95 days to maturity) is a good choice for the casual gardener, a broad-shouldered, rather small variety. Hollow Crown (105 days) has long roots but does well only in deeply prepared soils.

PLANTING SCHEDULE: Parsnips require a long spring to mature before summer heat since they will not thrive in high heats and droughts. In the South, plant seed in early spring for early summer harvests. In cooler regions, plant in mid-summer, for fall, early winter, for the following spring, harvests. Cover the row with peat, or a similar mulch that can be kept moist, to hasten germination.

PLANTING: Dig the soil well and mix with organic mulch and nutrients to a depth of 18 inches. As soon as the ground is soft, sow seeds in furrows ½ inch deep. Cover with ¼ inch soil. Roll or tamp the soil to improve germination. Mulch over the planting lightly when sowing in summer. Since they are slow sprouters, you can intercrop with radishes, or lettuce, or garden cress in spring plantings.

CULTURE: When parsnip seedlings are 3 inches high, thin to 3 inches apart.

HARVESTING: From late summer through fall, dig roots as needed. At the first sign of a hard frost, protect with coverings of old newspapers or organic mulch. The plants can stay in the ground through the winter in moderate regions, and be dug in early spring.

PEAS

Sow 4 seeds per foot
Germinates in 6–15 days
Do not plan to transplant
Matures in 60–80 days

SMALL GARDEN NOTES: Fresh-picked peas are one of the greatest delicacies the home garden offers, far superior to the peas sold by markets. Make room somewhere, even in the smallest garden, for either the climbing variety or the dwarf bush type. Peas go into the ground in earliest spring, and are up, harvested, and out of the soil in about 60 days, leaving room for the planting of flowers or food crops that will mature in summer or later. Climbing types will entwine a trellis, a support of string or wire, in any sunny spot and can be encouraged with string leads to go up a fence or any other tall stake. The low-growers, which produce on vines 6 to 18 to 28 inches long, can be planted early in borders of annual or perennial ornamentals, and replaced later with seedlings of flowering plants. Peas for drying—blackeye peas, also known as cowpeas and Southern table peas—are climbing vines. They can be eaten fresh, green, or picked and dried in the pods, shelled and stored for winter use. Cowpeas are less likely candidates for the small garden as they require quite a lot of room, and once dried are not noticeably better in flavor than dried peas sold for very little in supermarkets. Sugar peas— pod peas sold as Italian beans at the frozen food counters— are edible podded peas that have the qualities of fresh green beans and the sweetness of fresh peas. If you are looking for something unusual to grow in the small home garden, try a planting of dwarf sugar peas.

VARIETIES TO CONSIDER: For a long season of pea picking, a good choice is the climber plant Alaska, a standard smooth-seeded (the more wrinkled peas are sweeter) type. It germinates better than other varieties in cold, wet soil and is ready in a couple of weeks, before the sweeter types can mature. When the soil is drier, make succession plantings at 10-day intervals of dwarf types such as Burpeeana, Blue Bantam, Little Marvel—all ready in about 60 days. Wando, which requires 68 days to mature, and withstands heat better than the other varieties, can be planted 2 months before hot weather for a final harvest of peas. Among sugar, or podded, peas Dwarf Gray (65–68 days) is probably the earliest and the smallest, ideal for gardens where space is limited and the season is short. Blackeye peas for drying must not be planted before the danger of frosts has gone by. They go in last, and mature in upward of 60 days. Among desirable varieties are California Blackeye, Brown Sugar Crowder (85–90 days), and Blackeyed Peas, a dwarf plant that bears small, cream-colored peas with dark eyes.

PLANTING SCHEDULE: Smooth-seeded peas go in first, almost before frost is out of the ground; the wrinkled super-sweet varieties are planted 2 weeks later. Podded peas can be planted at the same time as the sweet varieties. The blackeye peas go in last, after all danger of frost is past. Repeated plantings of quick-growers after summer heat has gone by are desirable if you have the space, and if at that period in the summer, you have a 60-day stretch of growing weather ahead. Peas are definitely cool weather crops, and very difficult to grow well through the heat of summer, even when the varieties are said to be able to withstand heat. For a super-early crop of peas, prepare the soil in fall, and make the bed ready for planting. Sow seeds of the smooth-seeded type as soon as the ground is thawed (a week or two before it will be ready for working). With luck, the peas will produce a very early crop.

PLANTING: Peas (and beans) are legumes, and leave a supply of nitrogen in the soil so they do not require a heavy supply of this nutrient. Fertilize with a low-nitrogen fertilizer. In early spring, sow seeds of the earliest varieties, almost before the last frost is out of the ground. Plant seeds in trenches 4 inches deep, and 2 inches wide. Place seeds 3 inches apart and cover them with 1 inch of soil. Mulch the sides of planting but do not mulch over the seed. They need, at this cool season, all the heat they can get in order to germinate.

CULTURE: As the seedlings grow fill the trench with soil so the plants are well anchored and pull the mulch up to the feet of the plants.

HARVESTING: Young peas are sweet and tender. Pick them just after the baby stage, when the pod is swelling, but before its veins begin to coarsen. That is the way with all but the blackeye peas. Let those mature on the vine before picking.

POTATOES

Sow 1 piece per 18 inches
Germinates in 14–21 days
Don't plan to transplant
Matures in 80–100 days

SMALL GARDEN NOTES: Potatoes are a good choice for the small garden only if you are interested in seeing how this tuber grows, or if you have a passion for the small type of German fingerling potatoes found in Europe and in some specialty markets here. The fingerlings aren't baby potatoes but a special type that is small when full grown. Just to see how potatoes grow, cut up the sprouted eyes of left-over winter potatoes in early spring and plant them in a hill of sandy soil under a heavy mulch of spoiled hay: an occasional peek under the mulch reveals how the tubers develop roots that spread and in time produce tiny potatoes. You can plant half a dozen potato chunks almost anywhere in the garden. The plants that sprout from them grow to be 12 to 18 inches tall, have small pink-beige flowers and are an attractive enough green to take up a spot in the casual, ornamental bed. Planted in spring, they are over by mid to late summer, time enough to plant a succession crop of a quick-growing salad greens, or winter radishes.

VARIETIES TO CONSIDER: Any of the German fingerlings sold in specialty shops can be planted after they have sprouted eyes. The catalogs I have currently do not offer them for sale. Any regular potato that has developed eyes, as nearly all do by late winter, can be cut up and planted. Farm supply centers usually offer tubers for planting in areas where they grow well.

PLANTING SCHEDULE: Potatoes go in as early as mid-spring plantings in all areas, both early and later varieties. In the North, plant two types of potatoes, one for early summer use—Irish Cobbler, Early Gem, Norland, Norgold Russet, or Superior—and another to hold through winter—Katahdin, Kennebec, Chippewa, Russet Burbank, Sebago. In the Great Plains states, Pontiac and Red La Soda are planted for early crops, Katahdin and Russet Burbank for late harvests. In the Pacific Northwest, the Russet Burbank, White Rose, Kennebec and Early Gem are used, and in the southern states, Irish Cobbler, Red La Soda, Red Pontiac and Pungo are recommended by the USDA.

PLANTING: Potatoes grow well in nitrogen-rich soil. However, they don't like sweet soils so don't plant where soil has been recently limed or where ashes or fresh manure have been added. After the last frost, plant cut-up potato pieces, two eyes to a piece, eyes up, 18 inches apart, in trenches 4 to 6 inches deep, and cover with 2 inches of soil or with 6 inches of mulch, such as spoiled hay.

CULTURE: Potatoes send up shoots in 2 to 3 weeks. When seedlings reach 5 inches, hill the earth up around each to a depth of 2 inches and pull mulch up around the plants to discourage weeds. If mulch is the only covering used, keep its depth consistent—it tends to shrink or wilt as it dries.

HARVESTING: Dig potatoes from the time the vines start to wilt, until the vines are dead. Dig carefully so as not to spear them with the spading fork. Work each hill well. It's easy to miss potatoes. Leave them to dry in the field for a day, then pack in bushel baskets or burlap bags. Dark, humid places with a temperature of about 45 to 50 degrees are ideal for storage. Before the potato tops mature and begin to wilt you can dig baby potatoes for table use. However, potatoes dug before the tops mature do not keep well.

RADISHES

Sow 14–16 seeds per foot
Germinates in 3–10 days
Don't plan to transplant
Matures in 20–60 days

SMALL GARDEN NOTES: There are two types of radish: small, mild, quick-to-mature types for early spring planting, and large, strongly-flavored winter radishes that mature in autumn. The first type makes a delicious first-course dabbed with butter and eaten with crackly French bread. The winter radishes are best sliced thinly into salads, or used as long, thin strips in Oriental dishes. For the small garden, spring radishes are easy to grow, because they are ready so soon. Use them as a marker crop and companion planting for slow seeds, like those of carrots, or as a first crop for soil destined for a late spring planting. They mature in something over 20 days depending on the warmth of the season.

VARIETIES TO CONSIDER: Among the quick growers—22 days more or less—are varieties such as French Breakfast, Cherry Belle, Scarlet Globe, and Red Boy. For a continuous crop, you can plant these simultaneously with early types such as Champion (about 28 days to mature) or Crimson Giant (29 days). Among good fall and winter radishes are Long Black Spanish and White Chinese. They go into the ground in late summer when you still have 60 days of growing weather ahead.

PLANTING SCHEDULE: As soon as the ground can be worked, sow a half package of the quick growers, and half a package of a type that take 28 days to mature. Ten days later repeat these sowings and you'll have fresh radishes through late spring. In the cool of late summer, plant the winter types. They'll need 2 months to mature, then you can store the roots in damp sand in a cool spot sheltered from frosts, and you'll have radishes through early winter.

PLANTING: Sow seeds broadcast over dug and raked soil. Sow the seeds in a row, a circle, or in whatever pattern you like, leaving an inch or two of space between seeds. Cover with ¼ inch of fine soil and tamp firmly. No mulch is needed as the seeds will be up and the crop harvested before weed season gets underway. Water after sowing to encourage quick germination.

HARVEST: When the shoulder of the radish pokes out of the soil, the radish is ready to pull. As you pull the maturing radishes, you'll be leaving room for the slower seedlings to develop. Harvest ripe radishes promptly; radishes kept in the ground too long turn woody and tough.

RHUBARB

Matures the second season

SMALL GARDEN NOTES: Rhubarb is an excellent choice for the small garden because it is an attractive plant. It maintains its red stems and handsome dark-green leaves all season long, and it shoots up creamy white spears of florets after the picking season has gone by. It is a perennial—that is, it grows back year after year—and can go into the perennial flower border or among foundation plantings if the soil there isn't too acid. Or, set rhubarb as a clump anywhere that a planting the size of low shrubs is desirable. It can also be grown in clumps in large, deep containers. Rhubarb is best suited to areas having cool, moist summers and winters cold enough for the ground to freeze several inches deep. Four to six plants will supply all the average family can use fresh. The leaves, by the way, are injurious—don't eat them!

VARIETIES TO CONSIDER: MacDonald, Valentine, and Victoria (whose stalks are greener) are standard varieties.

PLANTING SCHEDULE: Rhubarb planted this spring must not be harvested before next year and should not be heavily picked until the third year. Plant roots are sold by catalogs and local garden centers in early spring. In areas where the winters aren't too severe, you can plant in late summer.

PLANTING: Dig holes 3 to 5 feet apart each way and 10 inches deep. Add a mix of rotted manure or compost and dried manure, or commercial fertilizer and humus, to the soil in the bottoms of holes. Cover with 2 inches of loam. Then place the rhubarb roots so each crown is 4 inches below the soil surface. Water. Fill the hole with loam and tamp gently. Pick a permanent location: once established rhubarb will grow for 8 to 9 years, or more, with little care.

CULTURE: Each fall, work a small handful of manure into the soil around each plant or mix in 2 tablespoons of garden fertilizer. A handful of ashes from the fireplace spread around each plant in very early spring improves growth. Dig up the clumps every 6 to 8 years, halve, and transplant.

HARVEST: In early spring, when the plant has a full stand of lovely pink-green stalks, it is ready to harvest. Pick large stalks from outside of clump. Twist slightly, and stalks will come free of the base. Don't cut stalks. Harvest *only* in early spring.

STRAWBERRIES

Harvest the second season

SMALL GARDEN NOTES: Strawberries are a good choice for the small garden, because they can be set in so many places (they are excellent subjects for container gardening) and because the crop is such a delicious luxury. For the gardener who has little space and little time for food gardening, they're a natural. Place the big standard varieties in rows in a stepped garden, or in any container where a border of serrated green leaves will be attractive or at the feet of containerized dwarf fruit trees or in a window box (but it should be big so you can have a worthwhile crop.) Place the smaller type called "wild" or *fraises des bois* as edgings along ornamental borders. They are offered in everbearer varieties, plants that produce some fruit all season long, and the twinkle of red fruit and white blossoms among the delicate leaves is truly delightful. Strawberries are perennials. The beds produce best when they are reset every few years as described below. The standard varieties give one crop each season.

VARIETIES TO CONSIDER: A variety now offered as Alexandria grows to maturity from seed the first season. Any number of standard (one crop) varieties are offered by catalogs and local garden centers. It is wise to let your garden center recommend a variety suited to your area. There are many everbearers offered, too. Well-known ones include Hartzland, Alpine Yellow, Ozark Beauty. For a succession of harvests, try these continuing varieties: Blakemore (extra early), Premier (early), Sparkle (midseason), Fairfaz (early), and Superperfection (everbearer). Or other varieties offering a similar succession.

PLANTING SCHEDULE: Plant strawberry plants in early spring, as soon as the ground can be worked. Plan to keep the flowers picked the first season to avoid the setting of fruit. You can harvest the second year. Suppliers suggest the harvesting of fruit from everbearer types the first season. Go ahead— but I still think it's better to wait until the second year.

PLANTING: Since strawberries require slightly acid fertile soil, dig a half shovelful of acid humus into the soil for each plant (peat moss, sawdust, cottonseed meal or leaf mold), plus a handful of 5-10-5 or 4-8-4 for each 20 feet of row. An alternate method is to dig a 2-inch covering of well-rotted manure or compost into the bed plus a good supply of fertilizer. As soon as the ground can be worked in early spring, plant the strawberries. Do not allow the roots to be exposed to the sun while waiting to be set in the ground. Make a furrow 1½ inches deep and 4 inches wide. Crowns must be at the exact level they grew before, not higher, not lower. To get this just right, hold plant by its center stem, level with the surface of the earth, spread the roots out over a small hump in the trench floor, and cover with 1¼ inches of soil. It is important to tamp the soil well, so that no air pockets are left near the roots. If frost threatens, protect plants by covering with plastic bags or bushel baskets.

CULTURE: During the first season pick all blossoms. Do not give in to the temptation of an immediate crop of juicy straw-

112

berries. If you religiously nip off the buds this year, the second year's crop will make the wait worthwhile.

If you let them, the plants will root runners, forming new matted rows. If you prefer, you can cut the runners from parent plants and set them in straight new rows yourself.

Regardless of the method you follow, in 4 to 6 years the bed must be dug up. Two years before the bed must be changed, root as many runners as you want for a new bed. Transplant during the following spring. Thus you can clear the old bed while picking berries from the new bed.

Once the winter temperature is in the low 20s, cover the bed with 6 inches of mulch; when the ground freezes hard, add a foot of mulch. Remove most of the mulch in early spring, so the sun can warm the ground. Second season, feed the beds in early spring with 5-10-5, at the specified rate at a time when the leaves are completely dry. Don't let any fertilizer get on the leaves; if it does, brush off immediately, a feather duster is a good tool. Then water in the fertilizer. An easier method is to water the row with a liquid fertilizer that will not hurt the leaves.

HARVESTING: The second season, pick berries as they ripen; they are ripe when plump, brilliant red, and the skin has a satiny sheen. Pick them promptly because ripe ones quickly become overripe if allowed to stay on plants. Harvest berries in a non-metal container.

TURNIPS

Sow 6–8 seeds per foot
Germinates in 5–10 days
Don't plan to transplant
Matures in 30–60 days

SMALL GARDEN NOTES: Small white turnips, home-grown and just picked, are a delicious spring crop. In the open garden, they require a fair amount of row space to mature, but you can grow them for picking baby-size in containers or stepped gardens or even in a bushel basket.

VARIETIES TO CONSIDER: For the small garden or con-

Growing turnips in a bucket.

tainer growing, select early varieties such as Tokyo Cross, a hybrid that matures in about 35 days. Harvest when 2 inches in diameter, or leave in the row to mature at 6 inches. Early Purple-top Milan is another quick turnip, mature in about 45 days. It is a home garden favorite, best harvested when 3 to 4 inches around. Foliage, or Shogoin Turnip, has edible foliage ready in 30 days, and a root that is ready in about 60 days—a double harvest.

PLANTING SCHEDULE: You can have two turnip crops, one that goes into the ground in early spring, and comes out 30 to 40 days later, leaving space for crops to be planted in mid-spring. Another crop can be planted in summer when you have 45 to 60 growing days ahead. Plant yellow turnips (see Rutabaga.) for turnips to store for winter.

PLANTING: Sow turnip seeds as soon as the ground can be worked, in drills 1 inch deep and cover with ½ inch of soil. Tamp, water, and mulch between rows.

CULTURE: When the seedlings are 3 inches tall, thin them to stand 2 inches apart if they are to be picked at baby-size,

114

and 4 to 6 inches apart if they are going to be allowed to mature in the row.

HARVESTING: The early varieties will be ready for harvest as baby turnips in about 25 days from planting if the season is warm. Pick the first to show shoulders through the soil, leaving room for the others to grow. Pull turnips gently by their tops. If they don't come away easily, use a spading fork, or a trowel, to lift the clump holding the turnip. Young turnip greens are often good, even those of turnips not sold for their foliage.

The table below is a rundown of the food plants to be set into the ground in early spring. The proposed spacing between rows and plants is that considered optimum for vegetables and fruits growing in a fair-sized open garden. If you want to save space, follow instead the recommendations in each individual entry for space to be allowed between rows and plants.

EARLY SPRING PLANTING

(As soon as the ground can be worked)

Vegetable	Space between rows (inches)	Space between plants (inches)	Depth to plant (inches)	Plants per 25 foot row
Asparagus (perennial)	48	18	8–10	17 plants
Beets	12–18	2–3	1	¼ oz.
Broccoli	20–24	18	1	½ pk.
Brussels Sprouts	20–24	18	1	½ pk.
Cabbage	20–30	18	1	½ pk.
Carrots	20	1–2	½	⅛ oz.
Cauliflower	20–24	18	1	½ pk.
Chard	18	6	2	¼ oz.
Chicory	12	4	½	¼ pk.
Cress	24	12	½	½ pk.
Dandelions (perennial)	18	4	½	¼ pk.
Jerusalem Artichokes (perennial)	48	18	3	1½ lb.
Kale	12–18	10–12	½	¼ pk.
Leeks	10–12	2–3	¼	1 pk.
Lettuce	12	2–4	½	½ pk.
New Zealand Spinach	24–36	12	½	¼ pk.
Onions	6–12	8	1	¼ lb.
Parsnips	12	3–4	½	1 pk.
Peas	18–24	3	4	¼ lb.
Potatoes	24–36	18	4–6	1½ lb.
Radishes	12	1–2	broadcast	1 pk.
Rhubarb (perennial)	36	36	10	8 roots
Strawberries (perennial)	36	12	1½	18 plants
Turnips	18	2–6	1	½ pk.

Chapter Six

PLANT THESE IN MID-SPRING

Early spring is defined as soon as the ground can be worked and responds to the snowball test. Mid-spring is the season between the time the ground begins to warm and the time the temperature climbs to 70 degrees and stays there. These plants are suggested for mid-spring planting because they may succumb to light frosts and won't germinate, or if they germinate won't thrive in the heavy, cold wet soil of early spring. I have tried to get a head start by planting seeds in early spring and found that they just didn't begin to flourish until the ground had warmed—no head start program at all.

You can, however, start any number of these plants indoors, and be ready to set out 3- or 6-inch tall seedlings by the time the ground has warmed. That constitutes a real head start program. Each entry that follows has a note about when seedlings started indoors can be transplanted. Most plants are ready to transplant between 4 to 7 weeks after the seed has been sown. Early varieties of fast-growing plants are ready in 4 weeks. Midseason varieties of slower growers take up to 7 weeks.

ARTICHOKES

Harvest the second season

SMALL GARDEN NOTES: Artichokes are tender ornamental perennials. (There are artichoke varieties sold purely for ornamental use.) The plants are the size of a small shrub, and very attractive. They look well in containers, or anywhere in the garden. Planting them in containers is recommended in areas where winter temperatures go below zero, because then they can be brought indoors to the cool, dry shelter of a garage or the basement for the winter. Generally, they are most successful in humid, foggy seashore climates where temperatures stay moderate throughout the winter. Six to ten plants will supply all you can use.

VARIETIES TO CONSIDER: Artichoke Grand Vert is a half-tender variety currently offered by catalogs, and a few dealers offer varieties billed as hardy. How hardy they really are is dubious—give yours winter protection, and don't try to grow artichokes if you live in the far north.

PLANTING SCHEDULE: Set out artichoke plants after the ground has warmed. Plan to harvest heads the second season. Give these somewhat tender plants the first season in which to establish themselves.

PLANTING: Make individual holes or trenches 8 inches deep, and mix into the trenches 2 inches of dried manure, rotted manure, or peat and fertilizer at the rate prescribed by the package. 5-10-5 is a good fertilizer for most soils meant for artichokes. This preparation is important, because the artichoke is a perennial which must bear year after year and so requires a good supply of food. Plant the roots 5 to 6 inches below the surface of the soil, cover with 4 inches of soil, and when the shoots are up, fill the rest of the trench with soil. When the plants are 4 inches tall, mulch well.

CULTURE: When the plants are 8 inches tall, cut away with a sharp knife all but six of the suckers that develop at the base of each plant. You can transplant these suckers to wet, damp sand to start a new set of plants. Halfway through the season, scratch a small handful of fertilizer, compost, or rotted manure into the ground around each plant. In the fall, cut the plants back to the ground, and in cool regions protect their roots with a bushel basket filled with leaves, or mulch. If the plants are growing in containers move them to the shelter of a cold frame.

HARVESTING: The edible part of the plant is a rosette of thickened bracts which surround the developing flower (the choke, or inner, part). The fleshy stem from which the flower grows is also edible (if peeled and boiled), so cut the flowerhead away from the branch 2 to 3 inches below the head.

BEANS

Sow 4–8 seeds per foot
Germinates in 6–14 days
Don't plan to transplant
Mature as shown below

SMALL GARDEN NOTES: Fresh green beans, 5 or 6 inches long, are among the most delicious of home garden crops, and the sweet, tender yellow wax beans are a close second in flavor and make a nice change in the menu. Though this is not a particularly ornamental plant and really doesn't fit too well into the flower border, it is such a desirable staple, that you should make room for a row either in a small open garden, a stepped garden, or a container garden. Beans, like peas, are grown in dwarf bush varieties or as vines that can climb trellises, good if the only space you have is overhead. Beans for drying are not particularly recommended for the small garden. They take a lot of space, are long to mature, and once dried, not so noticeably better in flavor than packaged dried beans sold commercially. Fresh lima beans are a delight (if hard to shell) but worth finding space for if you are a gourmet.

VARIETIES TO CONSIDER: Golden Wax is offered by most catalogs, a profuse bearer that is stringless and of good flavor. Kinghorn Wax is a good bush variety. Tenderpod and Tendercrop are popular bush varieties of green snap bean and endure more adverse weather than some other varieties. If bean mosaic and mildew are problems in your area, choose resistant varieties such as Tendercrop, Wade, Improved Tendergreen. These mature in 55 to 60 days from seed. Brownseeded, or white-seeded Kentucky Wonders are recommended as the best pole varieties for snap pod beans. These mature in 60 to 65 days. Lima beans come in pole and bush varieties, and the bush varieties such as Henderson Bush Lima and Baby Fordhook Bush Lima require 65-75 days to mature.

119

Fordhook 242 is heat resistant, indicated for the South and Burpee's Improved Bush Lima is a new variety, easier to shell than most. It matures in about 75 days. Pole lima bean varieties such as Prizetaker mature in about 88 days, and the Carolina, or Sieva, in about 78 days.

PLANTING SCHEDULE: Succession plantings of bush green or wax beans made every 2 weeks from the time the ground first thoroughly warms until 7 or 8 weeks before frost will give you season-long harvests. In the lower South and Southwest, bush beans may be grown in cooler seasons, during fall, winter, and spring, but won't do well in summer. Plan on one crop of pole beans only; the plants produce for weeks.

PLANTING: Drop bush bean seeds 3 inches apart in furrows 1½ inch deep, and cover with 1 inch of soil. Tamp firmly and mulch along the sides of the row. Sow seeds for pole beans in

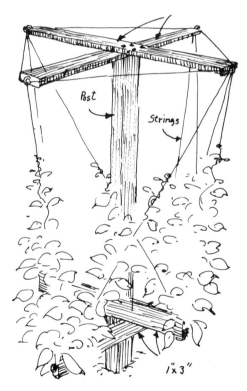

Permanent staking for pole beans.

120

hills 2 to 3 feet apart, six seeds to a hill, 1 inch deep; cover with ½ inch soil.

CULTURE: Bush beans growing in well-fertilized garden soil won't need further fertilizing, unless repeated sowings are made in the same row. In which case, fertilize the soil before each planting. Pole beans benefit from fertilizing when the blossoms appear. Work 1 tablespoon of 4-8-4, or your complete garden fertilizer into the soil in each hill. When pole bean seedlings are 3 inches tall, thin so that only four remain on each hill.

HARVESTING: Never pick snap beans when wet—you'll knock off blossoms that would have become the next beans to mature. Pick the snap beans when 5 to 6 inches long—that's when flavor is optimum. Don't let them grow longer than 8 inches or they will disappoint you. Keep ripening beans picked to encourage production. If they go to seed, the plant will stop producing sooner. Wax beans are best harvested after they turn a buttery, rich yellow. Pole beans to be used as fresh beans should be picked before they fully swell, just as they are becoming round. When shell-bean pods turn yellow, they are ready for harvesting, drying, and storing.

CELERIAC

Sow 8–12 seeds per foot
Germinates 9–21 days
Transplant in 10–12 weeks
Matures in 120 days

SMALL GARDEN NOTES: Often called turnip-rooted celery, this is a root vegetable with a celery flavor, fun for the gardener interested in trying something new. Started in early spring from seed, it matures in 120 days—and so must go into a garden that has room to spare. One package produces hundreds of plants, so share the package with gardening friends.

VARIETIES TO CONSIDER: Alabaster is a variety offered by many dealers.

PLANTING SCHEDULE: Seeds go into the ground after it has warmed, and it will take 3 months to mature a crop. This means celeriac will occupy its row all summer and give a crop toward early autumn.

PLANTING: Make furrows ¼ inch deep, water them lightly, and drop the seeds into the furrows. Cover with a dusting of fine soil. The weather and wind will fill the trench to ground level.

CULTURE: When the seedlings are 2 inches tall, thin to stand 6 inches apart. As the plants grow, rake the soil up around the tops until they are mounded 2 inches high above the ground level. After thinning, work a handful of 4-8-4, or your complete fertilizer, into the row.

HARVESTING: Roots have the best flavor when they are 2 or 3 inches around. Fully mature, they'll be about 4 inches around. To harvest, pull the roots up gently by the tops. If they resist, loosen the soil slightly with a spading fork. After the roots have been harvested, remove the side shoots, twist off the tops, and store the roots for winter in moist sand in a cool place.

CELERY

Sow 3–4 seeds per foot
Germinates in 9–21 days
Transplant in 10–12 weeks
Matures in 120 days

SMALL GARDEN NOTES: Celery is a plant to select for the small garden when you have space to spare for the many weeks required for it to mature and when you want to grow something most of your neighbors don't. The flavor of fresh celery is nice but one of its defects as a subject for the small garden is the fact that a lot more matures than you really want at one time. Though it keeps well refrigerated, not everyone has space, or the desire, for dozens of celery heads. If you are interested in celery, I suggest you grow a dozen plants in a space somewhere toward the center of the ornamental bed or in a container in an unused, sunny corner.

VARIETIES TO SELECT: Golden Detroit, Summer Pascal and Golden Plume are early celeries ready to be harvested during late summer and early fall.

PLANTING SCHEDULE: In the lower South, plan on celery for winter culture. In the upper South and in the North, plan on a late fall crop, and plant the seed toward early summer. You can keep some fall celery in the garden through early winter in mild regions by banking the plants with a few inches of earth and covering the tops with leaves or straw.

PLANTING: Plant in very fertile soil, well-supplied with organic matter supplemented by liberal additions of fertilizers. Before planting, to hasten germination, soak the seeds overnight in warm water. Make furrows ¼ inch deep, water the furrows lightly, and sow the seeds 4 to 6 inches apart. Cover with a dusting of fine soil, and tamp firmly. Or, cover the seeds with fine, damp leafmold, and cover that with damp burlap to encourage the seeds to sprout. Or, sow seeds indoors in flats and transplant to the garden when the weather has warmed. Set seedlings 6 inches apart in the rows.

CULTURE: When the plants are 8 inches tall, fertilize with 1 tablespoon of quick-acting nitrogenous fertilizer and hill the soil up against the stalks at a level just above the heart of the plant. Raise the hill every 10 days until the plants are 12 to 18 inches tall. Keep the rows free of weeds, either by heavy mulching or by weeding.

HARVESTING: Cut celery 2 inches below ground level (not hill level) and trim away the outer stalks.

CORN

Sow seed 1–2 per foot
Germinates in 6–10 days
Don't plan to transplant
Matures in 75–105 days

SMALL GARDEN NOTES: Regular sweet corn grows to be 6 to 8 feet tall, or more. Finding a spot where it will look well in the small garden isn't always easy. Furthermore, it isn't ready to harvest until late summer, so it is a season-long feature you have to hide, enjoy, or do without. Midget corn stands half this size, and is fun to grow for the sake of growing corn. But the tiny ears are only suitable for cocktail eating or pickling, and are not the big sweet ears we wait for each year. Indian corn, ornamental corn with kernels of many colors, and corn for popping, pose the same size problems as sweet corn. However, just once, sacrifice aesthetics to your taste buds and grow a stand of sweet corn. Picked when the kettle is already boiling and cooked in 8 to 10 minues, it is just about the best thing you ever tasted—far superior to even those excellent ears of fresh-picked corn sold by garden stands. Corn is one of the vegetables which most quickly converts its sugar to starch after picking. That's why your own garden-grown, just picked, corn tastes better than any other corn. And, just once, you should grow popping corn as a family project—children get such pleasure from popping corn they grew themselves. Because corn grows slowly and grows tall, it's a good idea to use the space around the plants for a companion crop—a low-grower such as pumpkin, squash, lettuce.

VARIETIES TO CONSIDER: My all-time favorite is Honey and Cream Sweet Hybrid, whose kernels are a mix of white and gold. The white corns have excellent flavor, too. Rainbow, (mixed colors in the kernels) and Strawberry Ornamental Corn (a pure deep red,) are sold by most dealers. Japanese Hulless is an excellent popping corn. Among midget varieties are White Midget and Golden Midget Corn.

PLANTING SCHEDULE: The standard corns require 75 to 80 days to mature, and only one crop is possible. The midgets mature a few days earlier. Popcorn requires 90 to 105 days, and the ornamental 105 to 110 days. In each case, only one annual crop is possible. In the South, sweet corn can be planted from early spring until summer, but won't do too well if it must mature during seasons of drought. In the North, sweet corn can be planted where early peas, beets, lettuce or other short-season, cool-weather crops grew before. Three plantings 10 days apart will provide a continuous supply in late summer for the garden with space to spare.

PLANTING: Plant corn in hills, groups of six, at the back of the garden. Corn requires cross-pollination, so blocks of the plants must grow together. Plant in holes 1 inch deep, five to a hill, 8 inches apart. Hills should be spaced 3 feet apart. Cover with ½ inch fine soil, tamp, water. Mulch around the hill. A low-growing companion planting of pumpkin, for instance, can be made at the same time and will mature in early fall.

CULTURE: When seedlings are 3 inches tall, thin to three plants per hill, and scratch a tablespoon of 4-8-4 or your complete fertilizer in around each hill. Keep weeds down with mulch (a companion planting can act as a mulch instead) and keep the plants watered when the corn is beginning to mature.

HARVESTING: When the silk begins to turn to brown, sweet corn is ready for harvesting. Plumped-out ears are ripe—you will have to watch them. First they are thin, then they begin to swell, then they plump out—that's the moment to harvest. Don't let ripe ears stay on the vine—they toughen. Popcorn and ornamental corn are ready to harvest when the ears have fully ripened. Pick them, strip back the husks and hang them in a dry spot to harden—this takes several weeks.

CUCUMBERS

Sow 3-5 seeds per foot
Germinates in 6-10 days
Transplant seedlings in the containers they grow in
Seed matures in 60 days.

SMALL GARDEN NOTES: Cucumber is a good choice for the small garden. It's a vine and can grow at the feet of almost any tall plant, ornamental or vegetable. It will climb trellising or string leads, covering them with broad pretty leaves in profusion. Grow in containers, stepped gardens, large window boxes, in boxes holding dwarf fruit trees, or in the open garden. The flavor of cucumber picked fresh when it is only 5 or 6 inches long is a delight. It's a very useful staple for summer salads. And it is fun to make pickles from cucumbers you have grown yourself.

VARIETIES TO CONSIDER: Cucumber seeds are offered in varieties for pickling or for eating. Varieties include those that grow extra long, thin fruits and some that grow lemon-shaped fruits. Pickling cucumbers are those described as "black-spined." They can be eaten fresh when small, or allowed to mature and then pickled. One of the nicest eating varieties is Burpless Hybrid, a long thin cucumber. Victory is a new hybrid that promises to resist the many cucumber diseases, but the seed of a pollinator (included with each package) must be used in each planting to guarantee fruit set.

PLANTING SCHEDULE: Start seedlings in peat pots indoors for an early crop (or buy started seedlings at the garden supply center) about 4 weeks before the ground warms. At the same time as you set out the seedlings, plant seeds in an adjacent hill—or another spot in the garden, to provide a cucumber harvest when the started seedlings have matured and their yield is running out. Cucumbers must be transplanted with their roots intact.

PLANTING: Sow five seeds to a hill in 1-inch deep holes, cover with ½ inch fine soil, tamp, water, mulch the hill well around the seeds. If starting seedlings indoors, plant two seeds ½ inch deep, to a 3-inch *peat* pot, and remove the weakest of the two before setting out. Cucumbers do not transplant well if lifted from their containers so plant container and all. Never start seedlings in flats, because then the plants will have to be cut apart and they'll sulk, and may die when transplanted. When setting out seedlings, plant four to a hill.

CULTURE: Thin seeded beds to four seedlings when plants are 3 inches tall. When plants are up, increase mulch and pull it up around the main stems to keep moisture in the ground. When watering cucumber hills, avoid wetting the leaves, as they are subject to diseases, and wet leaves seem more susceptible.

HARVESTING: Keep cucumbers picked as they reach 5 to 8 inches in length to encourage production and because that is the size at which texture and flavor is optimum in most varieties. Harvest only when the plants are dry. Pickling varieties may be picked at this size for eating fresh, or allowed to grow larger on the vine.

GOURDS

Sow 2 per foot
Germinates 7–10 days
Transplant in their containers or they'll sulk
Matures 10 to 12 weeks
Seed matures 100 days

SMALL GARDEN NOTES: Gourds grow on vines that will climb, and one or two hills will supply the average family with all the ornamental gourds they are likely to be able to use. Since they climb, they can occupy any vertical space the garden offers. The only caution with gourds is that they transplant badly; where they're planted is where they had better stay; or they must be transplanted in the pots they grew in.

VARIETIES TO CONSIDER: There are two basic types of gourds used as ornamentals—thin-shelled gourds which dry well and keep over winter, and edible, thick-shelled gourds which have fascinating shapes and colors but tend to mold after a few months. The thin-shelled gourds are not edible.

Turk's turban squash.

Generally they are sold in packets of mixed seeds. Edible, thick-shelled gourds include types called Lagenaria; Italian Edible Gourd and Italian Climbing Squash are varieties. The fascinating Turks Turban squash is sometimes used as an

127

edible (treat it as winter squash) and sometimes as an ornamental gourd.

PLANTING SCHEDULE: One crop of ornamental gourds is all you are likely to want. It goes into the soil in mid-spring as seed, and will be ready by mid-summer.

PLANTING: Plant six seeds to a hill, two seeds to a foot, in holes 1 inch deep. Cover with ½ inch of soil, tamp, water, mulch around the seed.

CULTURE: Thin to four plants to a hill when seedlings are 3 inches tall.

HARVESTING: Allow the thin-shelled gourds to ripen and dry on the vine if possible and allow them to dry thoroughly in a well-ventilated, warm, dry place before moving indoors or shellacking. If they aren't thoroughly dried, they'll mildew. Edible ornamental gourds should be picked for eating while still young and tender. Allow those intended for ornamental use to dry thoroughly on the vine and again indoors. Don't be disappointed if they don't last through winter in the arrangements they grace.

KOHLRABI

Sow 8–12 seeds per foot
Germinates in 3–10 days
Transplant in 4–6 weeks
Matures 48–60 days

SMALL GARDEN NOTES: Kohlrabi has a delicate flavor, a cross between young, fresh turnip and cabbage and looks a little like a flying saucer. All of which makes it fun to grow when you tire of the garden staples. The plants are small and close to the ground, not particularly pretty in the ornamental bed but easy to grow in fairly shallow containers. Half a packet can be tucked into an empty corner of the garden after an early crop is up and out.

VARIETIES TO CONSIDER: Early White Vienna and Early Purple Vienna are two varieties found in catalogs. The latter is a little larger.

PLANTING SCHEDULE: You'll only want one crop. Plant it after an early crop is up and out, and it will be ready in 55 to 60 days. In the North, it can be sown indoors for transplanting to the garden and will mature sooner. Or, the seeds can be sown where they are to grow. In the South, kohlrabi can be grown at almost any season except mid-summer.

PLANTING: Sow seeds in furrow, or holes, 1 inch deep, and cover with ½ inch of soil. Mulch around the seeds, water well.

CULTURE: When the seedling are 3 inches tall, thin to stand 6 inches apart. If planting started seedlings, plant 6 inches apart. Thinnings may be transplanted if you have space.

HARVESTING: The thickened base of the stem is the edible part, and it has the best flavor when 3 to 5 inches in diameter. Slice the bulb loose from the root just below the swollen base, and discard the rest of the plant.

PEPPERS

Sow 6–8 seeds per foot
Germinates in 10–20 days
Transplant in 6–8 weeks
Matures in 60–80 days

SMALL GARDEN NOTES: Peppers, the small and medium-sized hot peppers, and the big sweet bell peppers, are pretty plants 12 to 24 inches tall, that look well in the ornamental bed, or anywhere else you have a bit of space. Six plants will supply the average family with lots of sweet peppers for salads and six plants of the hot variety are more than enough for pickling. The small hot peppers will grow well indoors, and are attractive houseplants. The other two types can be grown in containers of all sorts: window boxes, stepped gardens, at the base of containerized larger plants, or in the open garden.

VARIETIES TO CONSIDER: Among good varieties of sweet, or bell, peppers offered by dealers are Penn Wonder, Ruby King, World-beater, California Wonder, and Yale Won-

Pepper plant growing in a bucket.

der. The varieties named Hungarian Wax, a medium-long pepper, and the small Long Red Cayenne, are hot peppers.

PLANTING SCHEDULE: Peppers require 65 to 75 days to mature and can be planted only after the ground has warmed and all danger of frost is gone. For gardeners in cooler regions, this means peppers should be started indoors 6 to 8 weeks ahead and set out as seedlings or purchased as seedlings at the garden centers. In areas where a longer growing season prevails after the ground has warmed, they can be set out as seed. Once the plants start producing, they continue to set peppers as long as the weather is fine, and as long as the maturing peppers are picked to encourage production.

PLANTING: Peppers are most successful in soils with a high sand content, but will succeed in heavier loams, too. Plant seeds in holes or trenches 18 inches apart and ½ inch deep, cover with ¼ inch of soil, tamp, water, mulch around the seeds, but not over them. Or, start seeds indoors, two to a 3-inch peat pot, about 6 weeks before planting time, and thin to one seedling per pot when the plants are 4 inches tall. Transplant container and all to holes dug in the garden about 18 inches apart.

CULTURE: When the plants are beginning to set fruit, work a tablespoon of 4-8-4, or your garden fertilizer, in around each plant, and keep the plant watered through mid-summer droughts.

HARVESTING: Peppers can be picked at any stage of maturity, but the sweet peppers when very small have thin walls and lots of seeds and aren't at their best. Pick instead when they have swelled to the size sold in markets. They can stay on the vine without losing flavor or freshness longer than other ripe fruits. Many varieties turn red when they are truly mature, but this usually has time to happen only in warmer climates with a very long growing season. To see the plants through the first early frosts, cover them with plastic bags or heavy paper bags. Chances are they'll still be producing through Indian summer.

PUMPKINS

Sow 2 seeds per foot
Germinates in 6–10 days
Don't plan to transplant
Matures in 100–120 days

SMALL GARDEN NOTES: One pumpkin vine can fit in almost anywhere, is easy to grow, and will produce half a dozen pumpkins—enough for display. Pumpkins are useful for more than pie-making and Halloween fun. Fresh pumpkin, seeded, peeled, cooked, and served as squash, has a delicate flavor. To have enough for use as a vegetable, to freeze for Thanksgiving pies and winter use, as well as for jack-o'-lanterns and fall display, plant half a dozen pumpkin seeds and thin to four sturdy seedlings. Pumpkins can be treated as a companion planting for tall, long-season plants such as corn. They can be grown over a compost pile, set to run along the base of a fence, in containers of all sorts; in fact, pumpkins grow easily in almost any space, anywhere, and they don't need as much sunlight as do most other food plants. Pumpkin seeds once sprouted and flourished on a pile of almost pure gravel in the shade of a giant pine tree in my yard.

VARIETIES TO CONSIDER: Small Sugar and Connecticut Field are among the orange-yellow skinned varieties, and require about 100 days to mature from seed. Big Max pumpkins, which have weighed in at over 70 pounds, need 120 days to mature. Cinderella, ready in 95 days, is a good choice for a small garden, and produces fruits 10 to 12 inches in diameter —nice for eating and ornamental display, but a bit small for jack-o'-lanterns. Jack-o'-Lantern, ready in 110 days, a variety of Connecticut Field, is considered excellent for Halloween carving. Striped Cushaw is a handsome type, a creamy white mottled with irregular stripes of green.

PLANTING SCHEDULE: Pumpkins are sensitive to cold, and can't be planted in the North until the ground has thoroughly warmed. In the South, they have trouble in midsummer. Plant only one crop. Set out in mid-spring, the pumpkins will begin to mature 3 months later, in early fall.

PLANTING: Plant two seeds to a foot in furrow 2 inches wide and 1 inch deep. Cover with ½ inch of soil, tamp, water, mulch around the seeds.

CULTURE: When the plants are 3 inches tall, remove the weaker of each pair of seeds. Hills of pumpkins containing one or two plants should be 5 feet apart each way, as this is a vigorous, big, bushy vine. When fruit begins to swell, keep well watered, and scratch a tablespoon of 4-8-4 or your own garden fertilizer, in around each hill to encourage big fruits.

HARVESTING: Pumpkins are harmed by hard frosts though they can withstand a little exposure to light frosts. When the fruits have brightened to full orange, and before real frosts set in, gather and store them where temperatures are about, or above, 50 degrees but not over 65, and where frosts cannot reach them. They can be set as ornaments in the lee of the entrance to your house, or by the garage wall if there's an overhang, on the porch, or in the shelter of a stone wall.

RUTABAGA

Sow 4–6 seeds per foot
Germinates in 3–10 days
Don't plan to transplant
Matures in 85–90 days

SMALL GARDEN NOTES: Rutabaga is sometimes called yellow turnip, but it is not a turnip. These long-season root crops aren't particularly recommended for the small garden, unless you are planning to grow a lot of vegetables of types that can be stored for winter. The small, fast-growing, and more delicately flavored turnip is a better choice for the small garden.

PLANTING AND CULTURE: See Turnip.

HARVESTING: Harvest, as turnips, by digging the roots at maturity, and before hard frosts set in. To keep, dip well-washed and dried rutabaga in melted paraffin and store for the winter in a cool place.

SALSIFY

Sow 8–12 seeds per foot
Germinates in 14–20 days
Don't plan to transplant
Matures in 120 days

SMALL GARDEN NOTES: Salsify is a root crop, one to consider for the small garden if you want to try something new. The flavor reminds me of oysters (it is sometimes called "vegetable oyster") and it is similar to parsnips in its growing requirements. Grow this in the open garden. Half a package will give you lots to dig and eat fresh, and some to keep over for winter.

VARIETIES TO CONSIDER: Sandwich Island is a recommended variety offered by many catalogs.

PLANTING SCHEDULE: Plant only one crop after the ground has thoroughly warmed. Plan to harvest in early fall and to leave some salsify in the rows with protection through winter for spring harvest.

PLANTING: Salsify will do best in light sandy soil. Prepare the soil well to a depth of 12 inches, and incorporate lots of organic materials. Sow seeds in furrow ½ inch deep, cover with ¼ inch soil, tamp firmly, water, mulch around the row. Germination is slow so mark the row with radishes or lettuce which will be up and out before the salsify can crowd these.

CULTURE: When the seedlings are 3 inches high, thin to stand 3 inches apart.

HARVESTING: Dig roots for immediate use from late summer through fall. When hard frosts threaten, cover the row with old newspapers or an organic mulch, and you can continue to harvest until hard frosts arrive. Salsify may be left in the ground over winter and dug for use in spring, or it can be lifted and stored in damp sand as other root crops.

SPINACH

Sow 4–6 seeds per foot
Germinates in 5–10 days
Don't plan to transplant
Matures in 40–50 days

SMALL GARDEN NOTES: Fresh spinach is a delicacy and a plant to consider for the small garden since it can be grown in containers and stepped gardens, as well as in the open garden. It has a couple of drawbacks. It is finicky about soils, and in rich clay it bolts almost before it is up. Muck soils are its favorite, but not everyone has muck soil and it isn't easily duplicated. Instead I plant New Zealand spinach, kale, or Swiss chard, which I find surer to be successful. However, I don't think any of these greens really equals the flavor of fresh-picked spinach.

VARIETIES TO CONSIDER: Long standing Bloomsdale is a recommended variety for sowing in spring. Virginia Savoy and

Hybrid 7 are resistant to downy mildew and indicated in areas where these problems prevail. These varieties are suited to late summer planting; planted in mid-spring, they may bolt quickly.

PLANTING SCHEDULE: In most of the cooler regions, spinach is an early spring, or late fall crop, but in areas of the South, it can be grown through winter. Where summer heat isn't too great, spinach can be sown as a continuous crop from early spring to late fall. Each seed yields one plant; each sowing, only one harvest, ready in 6 to 7 weeks.

PLANTING: Plant spinach in well-drained soil that has a high organic content to retain moisture. Do not plant in really acid soils, or lime to lessen the acidity. Sow seeds in drills, 4 to 6 seeds per foot, in furrows ½ inch deep, cover with ¼ inch soil, tamp firmly, water, mulch along the drill sides.

CULTURE: When the seedlings are 3 inches high, thin to stand 4 inches apart.

HARVESTING: To harvest, cut spinach plant off just below the spot where the stem branches out into leaves. Harvest only what you can use for one meal. Wash very thoroughly—sandy spinach is awful, no matter how nice the flavor.

SQUASH

Sow 1–2 seeds per foot
Germinates 6–10 days
Don't plan to transplant
Maturity—SEE BELOW

SMALL GARDEN NOTES: Summer squash produces for a long period through mid-summer, is delicious when picked small, and is one of the staples small gardens should make room for. Squash grows as bush and vine varieties. Bush varieties are best for the small garden, unless you want to grow the plants vertically, up fences, or horizontally, along the ground. Summer squash is not particularly decorative and I don't recommend it for the ornamental border. The good winter squashes, notably butternut and Hubbard, take up more

Pattypan squash.

space and require longer to mature but make excellent fall and winter vegetables. The winter types are vines, and like pumpkins can be sown as companion plantings for tall vegetables such as cabbage. Once the cabbage is harvested the squash can take over the row.

VARIETIES TO CONSIDER: Both the summer squashes called zucchini (long, green) and summer squash (shorter, plump, yellow) are worth finding place for. These are both crops to harvest in mid-summer. Other good varieties of summer squash include Early Golden Summer Crookneck (53 days), Cocozelle Bush, and Italian marrow (not unlike zucchini, 60 days), Early White Bush (a pattypan type, 54 days). Among winter squashes are Hubbard and Blue Hubbard (about 115 days to maturity), Buttercup (105 days) which has a turban shape and thick orange flesh, Hercules (88 days), a butternut type, Waltham Butternut, and Turk's Turban Ornamental Squash (100 days) (see also Gourds). Royal Acorn (80 days) and Table Queen Vine (85 days) are acorn types.

PLANTING SCHEDULE: For a long season of summer squash, plant half a package each of one of the yellow summer squashes and either zucchini or Italian marrow. Plant half of each half-package simultaneously and the remaining seeds of

136

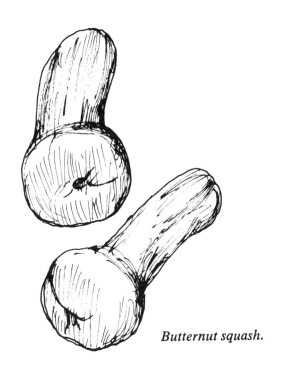

Butternut squash.

each 10 days later. At the same time, sow seeds for a selection of winter squashes. I suggest half a package, or less, of a butternut, and a quarter package of Blue Hubbard. These squashes will begin to mature when the summer squashes are going by and will continue to produce through fall. They can be gathered and stored for winter use when hard frosts threaten. In the South, squashes may be grown in the winter.

PLANTING: Plant bush varieties of summer squashes in drills, dropping two seeds to a foot of furrow 2 inches wide and 1 inch deep. Cover with ½ inch of soil, tamp firmly, water well, mulch along the sides. Plant fall and winter vine squashes in hills 5 feet apart, 6 seeds to a hill, in furrows as for summer squash.

CULTURE: When summer squash are 3 inches tall, thin away every second seedling. When winter squashes are 3 inches tall, thin to four seedlings per hill. Winter squash responds to a tablespoon of 4-8-4, or your garden fertilizer, scratched in around each plant after the vines begin really to run.

HARVESTING: Pick summer squashes when 6 to 8 inches long. The skin should be shiny and thin enough to penetrate easily with a thumbnail. Keep the young squash picked to encourage production. In fall, a few summer squash and zucchini left to stand under the vines through early frosts will develop into giants, excellent for braising, baking, or deep frying. Winter squash is best when fully ripe before picking. Butternuts aren't quite as good if picked when the skin still shows a tinge of green. Wait until it has turned buff-color all over. Pick winter squash as needed but let the balance of the crop stay in the field until hard frosts threaten. Store in a cool dry place for winter use.

TOMATOES

Sow 4–6 seeds to a foot
Germinates in 6–14 days
Transplant in 5–7 weeks
Plant matures in 40–80 days

SMALL GARDEN NOTES: Tomatoes are the most commonly grown of all the food plants in American gardens. The home-grown fruits taste good, are popular, are easy to grow, and give high yields per bush. Grow tomatoes anywhere: in baskets, in containers, in stepped gardens, window boxes, planters, on a sunny porch, in the open garden, in the ornamental bed or foundation border (as long as the soil is not acid). Six to 10 plants will supply the average family with more than they can use fresh, leaving some for giving, some for turning into tomato sauce and freezing or canning. The only drawback to tomatoes is that most types produce best if they are staked—but staking isn't a big chore.

VARIETIES TO CONSIDER: For a season-long harvest of tomatoes, plant some of the tiny tomatoes that grow in window boxes, pots, or anywhere: Pixie Tomato Hybrid is a typical example; it matures in about 52 days from seed, grows 14 to 18 inches tall, and has a heavy crop of tiny fruit 1¾ inches across. Small Fry Hybrid is similar. At the same time, plant some of the standard size varieties. These bushes are large, and mature

Simple ladder trellis for tomatoes.

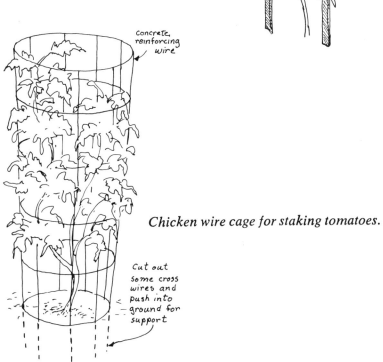

concrete
reinforcing
wire

Chicken wire cage for staking tomatoes.

Cut out
some cross
wires and
push into
ground for
support

Staking for container-grown tomatoes.

in 65 to 80 days. Among varieties recommended are Big Boy, Giant Hybrid, a very meaty tomato that is popular for flavor, and Beefsteak tomatoes, known as Crimson Cushion. If you want to try something new, consider Yellow Pear and Yellow Plum, small, mild, pretty fruits ready in about 70 days. Or try the large pink tomatoes noted for mildness, such as Globe, Oxheart, and Ponderosa, ready in about 83 days. Among large orange varieties are Jubilee and Sunray, ready in about 72 days.

PLANTING SCHEDULE: In most areas of the country, it is a good idea to start tomato seedlings indoors, 6 to 8 weeks before the ground will be ready to receive them. Starting your own seedlings allows you to be selective about the varieties you will grow. If you buy started seedlings at garden supply centers, you must be content with the varieties they offer. Plant the quick-to-mature tiny tomatoes so you'll have a crop in early to mid summer, a few of the standards, which will bear

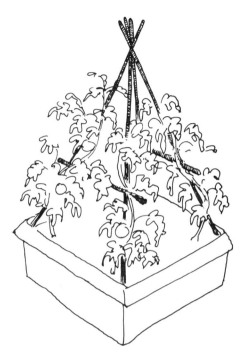

Teepee stake for tomatoes grown in a container.

from the time the tiny ones run out until frosts. Plant a few of the slow-to-mature giants and special types, such as Yellow Pear, to add variety to the menu.

PLANTING: The soil for tomatoes should be well-worked, and fertile. Plant seeds in peat pots or flats, 2 inches apart. Thin the weakest when the flat becomes crowded. Set seedlings in the open garden or in their outdoor container. In larger containers and in the open garden, or flower border, plant seedlings so they have 2 feet of space all around. Water, then mulch well around the plants.

CULTURE: A fertile soil speeds the maturation of tomatoes in my experience. So when the tomatoes have doubled their planting size, scratch a small handful of compost, or 4-8-4, in around each plant, and water well. Pinching out suckers seems to speed the setting of fruit, so follow the method shown in the sketch.

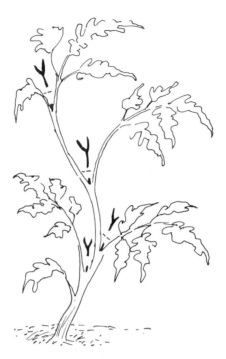

Pinching out tomato suckers.

STAKING: Staked plants produce better and more abundantly, but you can let tomatoes just trail along the ground if you like. They will still produce fruit, though some, late in the season, may be spoiled by contact with the ground.

HARVESTING: The flavor of tomatoes is best when they are dead ripe when picked. Dead ripe is when all the green at the base of the tomato has been replaced by full color. Keep the plants stripped of ripe tomatoes so they'll keep producing. Don't pick tomatoes when the leaves are wet. When the first frosts appear on the horizon, cover the tops with newspaper or sheets, and they'll still be producing when Indian summer arrives. When hard frosts threaten, pick all green tomatoes, wrap each loosely in newspaper, and set them in a dark, cool place to ripen. The tomatoes touched with white when picked green ripen well. Those that are really dark green when picked often rot before they ripen. Make tomato relishes with these.

The table lists the food plants to be set into the ground in mid-spring. The spacing proposed for rows and plants below is optimum for vegetables and fruits growing in a large garden. Suggested spacing for plants in small places will work in the open garden too, if you want to save space.

FOR MID-SPRING PLANTING
(As soon as the ground has warmed)

Vegetable	Space between rows (inches)	Space between plants (inches)	Depth to plant (inches)	Plants per 25 inch row
Artichokes (perennial)	36	36	5–6	9
Beans				
bush, snap	20–30	3–5	1–1½	⅛ lb.
pole	30–36	4–6 plants per pole	1	⅛ lb.
limas, bush	30–36	4	1–1½	⅛ lb.
limas, pole	30–36	4–6 plants per pole	1	¼ lb.
Celeriac	20	6	¼	⅛ pk.
Celery	20–24	6	¼	⅛ pk.
Corn				
sweet	36	8	½–1	⅛ lb.
Indian	24–36	10–12	½–1	⅛ lb.
popcorn	24–36	10–12	½–1	⅛ lb.
Cucumbers	48	4–6	1–½ (in peat pot)	¼ pk.
Gourds	36	60	1 (in peat pot)	¼ pk.
Kohlrabi	18	6–8	½–1	⅛ oz.
Peppers	20–24	18	½	18
Pumpkins (check turnips)	60	60	1	¼ pk.
Rutabaga	18	8	½	½ pk.
Salsify	12	3–4	¼–½	1 pk.
Spinach	18	4	¼–½	¼ oz.
Squash				
summer	24–36	6	1	¼ pk.
winter	72	60	1	¼ pk.
Tomatoes	3–4	2–3	¼–½	9
Turnips				

Chapter Seven

PLANT THESE IN LATE SPRING

A small group of garden vegetables can be set out only after the temperature outdoors is steady at, or above, 70 degrees. Some of these can be started as seedlings indoors. In cooler areas where there is a short growing season, plants like melon and eggplant must be set out as started seedlings if they are to mature crops before cool weather arrives.

EGGPLANT

Sow 8–12 seeds per foot
Germinates in 7–14 days
Transplant in 6–9 weeks
Matures in 60–75 days

SMALL GARDEN NOTES: Fresh baby eggplants sautéed in butter or pickled, are a gourmet treat. However, this is a warm weather plant very sensitive to the conditions around it. Eggplant requires a growing season of from 70 to 75 days or more, during which day and night temperatures must be high. Eggplant can be grown in northern gardens, if it is set out as a started plant and protected in the early and late days of its growing. It's fun to grow, however; a delicacy to

145

show off to gardening friends. You can grow eggplant in containers and in baskets. The plants don't take much space. If the soil is really fertile, less than half a dozen plants will produce as much fruit as you can use.

VARIETIES TO CONSIDER: Black Beauty matures in 73 days, and has very large fruits. Early Beauty Hybrid matures in only 62 days, and is a good choice for cooler regions. The plants produce small fruits over a long season. Jersey King Hybrid requires 75 days to mature fruits, and is taller than the other plants.

PLANTING SCHEDULE: Start this one indoors and plan to set out only after the nights are almost as warm as the days. In the South, eggplants are grown in spring and autumn. In the North only in summer. There is only one crop.

PLANTING: Sow the seeds indoors about 8 weeks before transplant time in peat pots or flats. Sow a dozen seeds, and cover with ½ inch soil. When the seedlings are grown, remove the weakest, leaving half a dozen to grow. It is important that these plants be kept growing without check, so don't let the flats dry out, and don't set them out to harden off until the weather is warm. After day and night temperatures reach 70 to 75 degrees, transplant to holes 18 inches apart in very fertile soil, water, mulch well around each plant.

CULTURE: Make sure the plants outdoor growth isn't checked by low temperature or dryness. Keep the mulch high around the feet of the plants to conserve moisture, and water well when droughts threaten.

HARVESTING: When fruit is 4 to 6 inches long and glossy black, cut through the stem about an inch from the base of the fruit. Keep ripening fruits picked so the plants will keep producing. When cold threatens in northern areas, shelter the plants under old blankets or a heavy covering of newspaper for all but the warm parts of the day.

MELONS

Sow 2 to a peat pot
Germinates in 3–12 days
Matures in 70–85 days

SMALL GARDEN NOTES: Muskmelons, the types called cantaloupe, are a really good choice for the gourmet gardener with little space. They'll succeed in containers and in the open garden. The flavor of the home grown varieties is very special. Though a warm-climate crop, melons can be grown in the cooler regions if the seedlings are started indoors and if trouble is taken to protect the plants at the end of the growing season. Melons growing vertically can ripen even heavy fruit if the fruit is supported on small shelves set beside each as it starts to swell, or in net bags pegged to the plant support. Melons are usually grown in the open garden and can be set at the feet of taller plants as long as sunlight isn't blocked off. They succeed in the climate and soil required for cucumbers, and except for the fact that they need a longer growing period to mature, aren't much more trouble. Honeydew melon ripened in your own garden is a special treat, but tricky to grow except in the West. Crenshaws mature in 90 days and are very large.

VARIETIES TO CONSIDER: Muskmelons require from 82 to 92 days to ripen. Some are orange-fleshed: Hearts of Gold, Hale's Best, Rocky Ford. Some are green-fleshed: Fordhook Gem, for instance. The Crenshaw melon offered as an early hybrid by many growers, is very large. It has a slightly different texture from the muskmelon, but when vine-ripened, the flavor is great, reminiscent of cantaloupe. It takes about 90 days to mature. Honey Mist, an early honeydew type (92 days) with greenish white flesh and extraordinary sweetness, is worth trying even if you aren't in the West. Among melons only for warm climates are the casaba melons, Golden Beauty, and a variety named Honey Dew. These take 110 to 120 days to mature.

PLANTING SCHEDULE: Start melon seeds indoors and transplant only after the temperature has steadied at 70 degrees or above. A dozen plants of mixed varieties will supply enough fruit for the average family. Make one sowing; the harvest will begin toward the late part of summer or in the very early days of fall. In the North, plan to baby the plants along in the late stages of development by covering them against cool night air with newspaper or old blankets.

PLANTING: Melons do best on light soils. Six weeks before planting time, start seedlings indoors in individual peat pots, two seeds to a pot. Cover with ½ inch of soil. Thin to the strongest seedling when the plants are 3 inches tall. When the weather has warmed, plant 4 peat pots to a hill, leaving 18 to 24 inches beween plants. Water well, without wetting the leaves, and mulch thickly.

CULTURE: Melons produce male and female flowers. You can tell the male flowers because the stem is slender, while the female flower has a thickened spot below the ovary. The female produces fruit. Pick off the male flowers after they have bloomed fully. Keep melons watered as the fruit begins to plump out, but avoid wetting the foliage as you water.

HARVESTING: You can tell that muskmelons are ready to harvest when the stem parts from the fruit with a slight pull. At this point, the netting on the skin of muskmelons is usually elaborate and slightly raised. Harvest at dead ripe for the best flavor. Melons you aren't ready to eat should be picked and stored in a cool, but not icy, place.

MUSHROOMS

Plant spores

SMALL GARDEN NOTES: Mushrooms reproduce by spores. The spores, planted by supplier, develop threadlike growths called "spawn" which are offered to home gardeners by catalogs. The home gardener interested in growing mushrooms in any real way, requires carefully prepared beds in a root cellar, cave, or a windowless room. You can try for a modest crop in a basement where moisture is high and temperatures can be kept at 54 to 68 degrees. Pasteurized compost as a growing medium is essential. Horse manure mixed with bedding straw is the traditional medium for the growing of mushrooms, though today some organic materials have been developed that are suitable. It is a complicated procedure to make your own compost. If you want to try, buy composted horse manure, or look for a manufacturer of organic supplies offering a suitable medium.

PLANTING

Broadcast mushroom spawn over the prepared bed of compost and spray the bed with a fine mister until it is about 70 percent soaked. Cover the spawn with a light layer of spoiled hay. In about a week, the spawn will send out mycelium. Cover the bed with an inch of sterile soil with a pH at about 7. The first mushrooms appear in clusters in 6 or 8 weeks. Imperfect ones should be removed before they fully develop. The matured mushrooms are cut from thin bases with a sharp knife daily and the spent bases are discarded. The average bed produces for about 3 months, then the beds are cleaned out and the process begun again.

For the average home gardener, a more practical way of investigating the phenomena of growing mushrooms is to buy seeded pots of spawn, now offered by many dealers.

OKRA

Sow 4 seeds every 3 feet
Germinates 10–14 days
Matures in 56 days

SMALL GARDEN NOTES: Okra, or gumbo, picked when tiny, is an excellent vegetable for the gourmet garden. It is a warm weather plant, sold in dwarf or larger growing varieties. Enough plants to yield a sampling of this southern staple can be tucked into container gardens or the open garden. Allow about 3 feet around for each plant. Okra is best tasting when it has been chilled, stemmed, covered with boiling water for 1 minute, then drained, before preparing for use.

VARIETIES TO CONSIDER: Among varieties recommended are Clemson Spineless, Emerald, and Dwarf Green. They take about 56 days to mature.

PLANTING SCHEDULE: Half a dozen plants set out after the weather has warmed will provide a good supply of okra 8 to 10 weeks later.

PLANTING: The soil for okra must be well drained. In cooler areas where crops must mature during a short growing season, the soil should be very fertile. Plant seeds in rows 2 or 3 feet apart, 4 seeds every 3 feet. Make the furrows 2 inches deep, and cover the seeds with ½ inch of soil. Weather will fill in the furrows. Water well, and mulch the sides of the rows.

CULTURE: When the plants are up and thriving, thin so they stand 18 inches to 24 inches apart. Pull the mulch up around the plants.

HARVESTING: Pick the pods while young and tender. Don't let any fully ripen on the vine or the vine will stop producing. Old pods aren't good and they exhaust the plant.

PEANUTS

Plant seeds 2 to a foot
Germinates 2-3 weeks
Matures in 110-120 days

SMALL GARDEN NOTES: Though primarily suited to culture in the South, peanuts give children such delight as a crop that the northern gardener who is a parent should try them. Peanuts grow easily enough anywhere in the open garden. They can be planted also in containers that allow several dozen seeds to grow with 8 to 10 inches between seeds in rows 2 to 3 feet apart. For small spaces, choose a dwarf variety.

VARIETIES TO CONSIDER: Jumbo Virginia (120 days) produces an extra large peanut and is suited to warmer climate. Spanish peanut (110 days) has small kernels and is a better choice for the northern gardener. It is a dwarf variety.

PLANTING SCHEDULE: Plant after the weather has thoroughly warmed. The nuts will be ready late in summer or in early fall. Light frosts won't harm the roots.

PLANTING: Plant hulled peanuts 8 to 10 inches apart, in furrows 2 inches deep, in rows 3 feet apart. Cover nuts with 1 inch fine soil, tamp, firm, water, and mulch along the rows.

CULTURE: Yellow pea-like flowers will appear on the branches and these will send out long, slender runners that dig into the ground. It is on these runners the nuts grow. Keep the plants watered during droughts.

HARVESTING: After the tops have dried in early fall, dig out the runners, and stack them in the garden to dry for several days. If rain threatens, bring them indoors. Hang the dried plants in a warm, airy place to finish curing, and pick the nuts as needed.

SWEET POTATOES

Start cut-up tubers indoors
Germinates 10 days to 2 weeks
Matures 120–150 days

SMALL GARDEN NOTES: Sweet potatoes are grown indoors for the vines which are decorative and the flowers they produce. They are not particularly recommended for the small garden outdoors as a staple, but are fun to experiment with if you have space to spare. Sweet potatoes are considered a Southern crop, but they will mature in climates that offer 150 frost-free days with relatively high temperatures. Started as cut-up tubers in small pots indoors and transplanted after the weather warms, sweet potatoes have a chance of maturing a crop in cooler regions. But this is not a particularly practical undertaking for the home gardener.

VARIETIES TO CONSIDER: Some varieties offered are Jersey Orange, Nugget, and Nemagold. These are types called dry-fleshed. Centennial, Porto Rico, and Goldrush are varieties of the type called moist-fleshed.

PLANTING SCHEDULE: In areas as far north as New York and southern Michigan, sweet potato tubers are set out in late spring, after the ground has thoroughly warmed and temperatures are staying in the 70's.

PLANTING: The soil for sweet potatoes should be deeply dug sandy loam, with moderate fertility. Where sweet potatoes are to be grown as a real crop, the tubers are bedded in soil in a hotbed, and covered with 2 inches of fine soil or sand. In the open garden, the sprouted tubers are set on top of ridges 3½ to 4 feet apart, with the plants 12 inches apart in the rows.

HARVESTING: Dig sweet potatoes shortly before frosts on a dry day and leave the tubers on the ground for 3 or 4 hours. The tubers grown commercially are cured after digging. Curing consists of setting them in a room with a temperature at 85 degrees for 10 days.

WATERMELONS

See Melons

SMALL GARDEN NOTES: The great big watermelons grown in the South are so readily available in that locale, that there seems little point in devoting space in a small garden to their culture. In the North they are a better choice for the small garden because they're not growing in every farm field. The only practical type for cooler regions is the midget watermelon now offered by most growers. Plant 4 or 5 seeds in large containers and let the runners spread..

VARIETIES TO CONSIDER: New Hampshire Midget Watermelon is typical of the dwarfs suited to shorter growing seasons. It matures from seed in about 70 days, and bears fruits about 8 inches long and weighing about 6 pounds each.

PLANTING, CULTURE, AND HARVESTING: See Melons.

The table lists the food plants to be set into the ground in late spring. Suggested spacing for rows and plants here is suitable for vegetables and fruits growing in a large garden. Suggested spacing for these plants as described in the previous pages put the plants somewhat closer together. You can space rows more closely in the open garden, too, if you want to save space.

152

FOR LATE SPRING PLANTING
(When the temperature stays above 70 degrees)

Vegetable	Space between rows (inches)	Space between plants (inches)	Depth to plant (inches)	Plants per 25 foot row
Eggplant	20–30	18	½	¼ pk.
Melons				
cantaloupe	48	18–24	1 in peat pot	¼ pk.
watermelon	72	36	1	½ pk.
Mushrooms	See entry, page **148**.			
Okra	20	18–24	½	1 pk.
Peanuts	24–36	8–10	2	1 pk.
Sweet Potatoes	24–36	18	5	1-1½ lbs.

Chapter Eight

HERBS IN SMALL SPACES

Even if you don't have an inch of real gardening space, you can grow herbs. They'll flourish in pots or boxes indoors, either on a sunny windowsill or under grow-lights. Container-ized herbs, singly or in groups, can be grown on the terrace of an apartment building, on the patio of an urban home, or in whatever small, sunny garden spaces may be available.

Herbs can be started indoors any time of year, and trans-planted to the outdoors or moved to a window box or terrace after the weather has thoroughly warmed. Most prefer an in-fertile and sandy soil. At the end of the season, the herbs can be potted up (cut back the tops by a third) and brought in-doors to window or light gardens. Most are from sunny cli-mates and won't withstand much frost. So if you are moving them indoors, do it before frosts hit.

Some of the herbs grow from annual seed, and some are perennial and will come back year after year. Many of the perennials are tender to the cold in northern areas of the coun-try. Treat them as annuals to be started from seed before each planting season. Because many of the herbs are slow to germi-nate, start them indoors early.

HARVESTING THE HERBS

You can pick branch tops or leaves for use fresh from any of the herbs at any time after the plant is flourishing. The best

A square 2 by 2 feet yields chives, sage, sweet basil, and loads of parsley. Keeping the tops picked keeps the herbs yielding through summer. (Photo by J. F. Michajluk.)

time to harvest leaves for drying and storage is when the flower buds are just beginning to open. Harvest as soon in the morning as the night moisture has left the plants and before the sun is hot overhead. You can cut away a third of each branch on a perennial without harming it. Annuals can be cut down completely, since they won't come back next year anyway. Or, cut them back by a third for drying use, and let the rest of the plant grow through the season for use fresh.

Lavender is an herb whose crop is the flowers. They are most fragrant before they open—so be sure to harvest them then.

The time to harvest herb *seeds*, dill seed, for instance, is

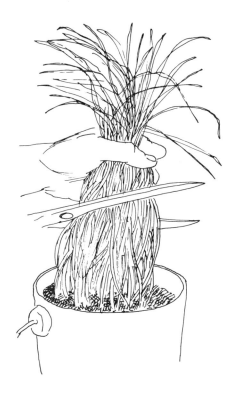

Snipping chive tops; they'll grow back.

after the flower stalks have dried late in the season. (Dill leaves, called "dill weed" in the dried state, can be snipped at any time in the season for use in salads or cooking.) When harvesting herb seeds, gather the seed heads into a basket or bowl and spread them on a clean, dry cloth to dry in an airy room. After 5 or 10 days, when the heads are bone dry, rub them between your hands over a bowl in a drafty spot—the draft will blow away the chaff—and let the seeds fall. Let the seeds dry another few days before storing in tightly-capped jars.

THE IMPORTANCE OF FULLY DRYING HERBS

Whether you are planning to store herb leaves or seeds, it is vital that they be bone dry, absolutely dry, before they are bottled. Otherwise, they will mildew or spoil and have a terrible flavor. Make sure the bottles they are stored in are absolutely dry too, and have air-tight caps.

HERB SIZE AT MATURITY

Herb	Height (inches)
Anise (annual)	24–36
Basil, sweet (annual)	12–24
Borage (annual)	18–24
Caraway (biennial)	24
Catnip (perennial)	36
Chervil (annual)	6–12
Chives (perennial)	10–12
Coriander (annual)	18
Dill (annual)	24–36
Fennel, sweet (annual)	6–10
Lavender (perennial)	24–36
Marjoram, sweet (annual)	12–24
Mint (perennial)	24–36
Oregano (perennial)	12–24
Parsley (biennial)	8–12
Rosemary (perennial)	36–72
Sage, garden (perennial)	24–36
Savory, summer (annual)	12–18
Sesame (annual)	24
Shallots (annual)	12–18
Sorrel, French (perennial)	36
Taragon (perennial)	36
Thyme (perennial)	6–8
Verbena, lemon (perennial)	48–60

PLANNING AN HERB GARDEN

An herb garden can be any size and any shape you have room for. To do an attractive plan for an herb garden, you need to know the height at maturity of each herb planned for it, so that the tall-growers can be set at the back of the herb border, or in the center of an herb wheel. The chart gives heights: use it to plan your garden.

PLANTING AN HERB GARDEN

Since many herbs are slow to germinate, start the herbs indoors as seedlings, following the general instructions accompanying the pictures in Chapter Four.

USEFUL HERBS FOR THE SMALL GARDEN

ANISE: An annual to start from seed. It has a licorice flavor often used in Italian and Mediterranean cooking, and sometimes in East Indian dishes. Use the leaves fresh in salads; the seeds in baking.

BASIL: Plant the variety called "sweet basil" (these are ornamental basils). Start the plants from seed, or buy them as started seedlings in garden supply centers. Keep the tops pinched out so the plants will bush out. Use the leaves fresh in Mediterranean salads and cooking, and with ripe tomatoes. A good indoor plant, and a "must" in the herb garden.

BORAGE: Start this from seed, in its own peat pots. Borage doesn't transplant well. It attracts bees, so if you have fruit trees requiring pollination, this is a good herb for your garden. The flavor is reminiscent of fresh cucumber. Use the fresh leaf in salads.

CARAWAY: This is a biennial that comes back the second year, but usually dies out the third season. If you want an annual supply, plant seeds close by the plant the second year for the following year's crop. Or, hope it will self-seed—it often does. Harvest seeds the second season and dry them for use in baking, in sauerkraut, with cheese. Grows well indoors.

CATNIP: The dried leaves of catnip seem to make cats dizzily happy, and often are used to stuff scratching posts (to encourage pussy to scratch the post, not the furniture). Catnip is also sold in little sachet-like pads to owners of cats. The plant is a perennial that reaches 3 feet in height and bears white or pale purple flowers in dense spikes; rather pretty. You can grow this from seed or from divisions of mature plants.

CHERVIL: Tastes like an exotic parsley, so plant it only if you have lots of room. You'l find parsley a more useful staple. Grows from seed. The leaf is excellent with egg dishes, salads, or fish. An annual that grows well indoors, too.

CHIVES: One of the most useful of herbs. The leaves look like, taste like, and are used in the ways fine onion are used. They grow, like onions, from bulbs. Chives don't do as well indoors as some other herbs, but a pot of it will last for several months on a sunny window. The plant throws up purple flowers which, by the way, are edible. Keep the flowers picked because if they go to seed, the plant will be weakened. Buy chives as started plants—or start a pot from seed.

CORIANDER: Useful, but less so than many other herbs. Grow it only if you do a lot of East Indian cooking. This is an annual to start from seed in its own peat pot. It won't transplant. Use the ripe seeds whole or powder them for use in breads, baking, or vinegar.

DILL: A wonderful herb for use in potato dishes, pickles, salads. It will grow well indoors. Start dill from seed in its own peat pot and transplant pot and all to permanent growing place. It won't transplant. Dill is one of the few herbs that seem to prefer rich soil. Use the ferns fresh in salads, with vegetables and meats. Dry seeds and leaves for winter use.

FENNEL (sweet): For the gourmet gardener. Fennel has a slightly licorice flavor, and is used primarily in Mediterranean dishes. Start the plants from seeds and follow the same general growing instructions as for celery in Chapter Six. Not for indoor planting.

GARLIC: Stand-by herb—not particularly recommended for indoor growing. The open garden is the best place for garlic, which grows from the "cloves" that form the head. Catalogs offer "garlic sets"—and indeed the cloves look very much like onion "sets." Organic gardeners plant garlic sets around, or near, plants needing protection from beetles and other pests. The strongly scented leaves seem to be a deterrent. Planting, culture, and harvesting is the same as that described under Onions in Chapter Five.

LAVENDER: This perennial is somewhat hard to start. It is a small shrub that will flourish indoors in good light if the air isn't too dry or hot. An herb to scent linens, it is pretty grown as a low hedge, and in old-fashioned herb gardens it was often used to outline the border. Lavender can be started from seed, but it is very slow to germinate. I recommend you buy it as a started seedling. Keep the tops pinched out to encourage bushiness. Harvest seeds the second season. Wood ashes from the fireplace dug into the soil around each plant in the early spring encourages growth. Once you have established plants, you can multiply them by rooting fresh, green tip-cuttings in damp sand in mid-spring.

MINT: There are dozens of mints, and most of them grow indoors. Peppermint is the strongly-flavored variety used for teas and for making jelly. Lemon, apple, orange, and pineapple mints are prettier plants with more delicate flavoring. You can buy plants as root divisions already started in peat pots, or beg roots from a friends' garden in early spring. Plant mints in containers; they tend to spread and will take over the garden if unchecked.

MARJORAM (sweet): Grows well indoors and can be started from seed, or tip-cuttings can be rooted in damp sand in early spring. This is a good plant to bring indoors as it does well in a sunny window or under lights. Use the leaves fresh in salads, vinegars, soups, egg dishes. Dry them for winter use.

OREGANO: Often called "pot marjoram," this perennial grows well indoors, too, or can be planted as a small hedge to be clipped annually. Nice in the rock garden, as it bears pretty purple or pink flowers. The leaves are used in many Mediterranean dishes.

PARSLEY: This is a biennial and probably the most useful of all the herbs for use fresh. Grow it in the herb garden, as a small hedge anywhere, in the flower border, or grow it in boxes on the patio, or indoors on the window sill, or under lights. Snip off branches at will. It will keep growing all season long. Grow parsley from seeds soaked overnight to hasten slow germination. The second year parsley will quickly go to seed, so sow new seeds nearby as soon as the parsley is up to provide a crop later that year and early the next year.

ROSEMARY: One of the taller herbs, and a tender perennial, this is a good one to bring indoors to the window or the light garden. Start rosemary from seed or from cuttings in early spring. Cuttings are better because rosemary so often is very slow to germinate. Use the leaf in Italian dishes, salads, soups, stews.

SAGE: A tall, and rather straggly herb, it must be kept pinched out at the branch tips. Sage is perennial, but tends to die out every 3 to 4 years. It grows well indoors within that time span however. In the open garden, it runs rampant over a small space, so grow it in containers. The dried leaf is used for stuffings; the fresh leaf, sparingly, in salads.

SAVORY (summer): An annual to start from seed, this, too grows well indoors, and does best on rich soil. Use the fresh leaves in salads, sauces, meats, stuffings.

SESAME: Not as commonly used as many other herbs, this is not particularly recommended for the small herb garden. An annual, start it from seed. The dried seeds are harvested for use primarily in pastries.

SHALLOTS: Tiny bulblets like onions with a flavor that is a cross between onion and garlic, but stronger than onion. Shallots are prized by gourmet cooks, and worth finding a little space for as they are very expensive to buy. Buy bulblets, and follow culture and planting instructions for Onions, Chapter Five.

TARRAGON: A tall perennial that dies in severe winters. Start this from cuttings, or buy started seedlings. Use the fresh leaves with grilled meats, salads, fish sauces, pickles.

THYME: A perennial which is a must in much European cooking and for fish soups and sauces, thyme is slow to germinate from seed, but will come back for years. You can start plants by rooting fresh, green, tip-cuttings in sand. The dried leaves are often used to deter moths.

VERBENA, LEMON: The dried leaves of this little perennial bush are a standard ingredient in most potpourri and sachet recipes. The plant can be started from seed, or from half-ripe wood cuttings in early spring. At maturity it will be 4 or 5 feet tall, so set it out as you would a small shrub. It grows well in containers outdoors and will grow indoors.

Chapter Nine

ORCHARD AND BRAMBLE FRUITS

The orchard fruits most suited to the small home garden include apples, pears, cherries and plums, peaches and nectarines. There are, of course, others: all the citrus fruits, but as these are grown commercially in most areas where they will grow at all, they are not an especially good choice if space is limited. The bramble fruits most suited to small gardens are those that appeal to the gourmet palate. Raspberries, a real luxury fresh or frozen (and they freeze beautifully when fresh-picked), are worth finding space for. If you have more space to spare, grow blackberries. They are excellent for eating fresh, and make wonderful jams, jellies, and pies. Blueberries must have acid soils. Since making alkaline soil acid is a year-in, year-out program, consider them only if you have suitable growing medium, or if you want to grow them in containers, or in an acid bed with evergreens.

Grapes are in a class by themselves, a good choice for the small garden, since they grow well vertically, and in containers, as well as in the open garden.

ORCHARD FRUITS

VARIETIES TO CONSIDER

APPLES: For the small home garden, select dwarf or semi-dwarf varieties of double red or yellow, Delicious, an apple that ripens in late summer and early fall, and keeps very well for winter. The flavor is wonderful; Grimes Golden is a dwarf that ripens a little later. Cortland, McIntosh, and Jonathan are tart fall apples, good for winter keeping; Red Staymen Winesap apples are smaller than the others, sharply-flavored and good keepers; Spritzenburg is a winter apple, good for pies; the Northern Spy, and Tompkins are among the best apples suited for jelly and pies. Not all dealers carry all of these in dwarfed varieties—you may have to look hard to find them. Many dealers offer five varieties of apple growing on one rootstock. I've never had luck with these curiosities, but others have, so try one if yours is a really small space. Many varieties of apple require cross-pollination, so make sure you select a pair of trees that will cross-pollinate. (See Chapter Two, table.)

CHERRIES: Cherries produce two distinct types of fruit—the big, black, sweet cherries, and the small, bright-red, sour cherries. The sweet cherries are best for eating, the sour cherries make the best cherry pies. Sweet cherries require cross-pollination (Chapter Two, table) to set fruit, so select two complimentary varieties. Sour cherries are self-pollinators. You need plant only one. Cherry trees are not too big for a small garden even at maturity, and any of the following varieties are good: Bing, with black fruit; Black Tartarian, black fruit; Kansas Sweet, with dark red fruit; Napolean with red-cheeked, yellow fruit; Yellow Glass, with bright yellow fruit. None of these are self-pollinators, but all, except Bing and Napoleon, will cross-pollinate each other. If you want to grow both Bing and Napoleon, you'll have to plant a third variety as a cross-pollinator. Dwarfs offered are Great New Northern Star and North Star, pie cherries that ripen fruit in July.

CRAB APPLES: Usually small trees with decorative fruit, these are a good choice if you like making jelly, but not especially suitable for eating. Hyslop is one of the best eating crab apples offered.

NECTARINES: A peach without the fuzz, is the nectarine. The trees are small and standard sizes are suited to limited gardening space. Surecrop is one good variety offered. An especially pretty tree, in spring it is covered with a mass of pink blooms.

166

PEACHES: Peaches are relatively hardy, and one of the dwarfest of the dwarf fruit trees. Many nurseries today offer trees that can be grown through maturity in containers suitable for the patio or terrace, or the roof garden. They are so small, in fact, you can grow an orchard of them in the few square yards, and harvest bushels of fruit. Elberta, Hale-Haven, and Golden Jubilee are among the varieties offered in dwarf form. Hale-Haven ripens fruit early in September, Elberta in mid-September, and Golden Jubilee, earlier, in August. Peach trees are not especially large, even in standard varieties, so consider any of the standards as potentially suitable for your garden. The varieties above are offered in standard sizes. One of the smallest of the dwarfs is Bonanza, and it is the peach best suited to growing in a container.

PEARS: Among the better dwarf pears are greenish Fame and Starkrimson, which bear in August. The Starking Delicious, Magness, Seckel, and Anjou ripen about a month later and are resistant to rust. The Duchess and Bosc pear ripen in December, where climates are moderate. Bartlett and Clapp's Favorite also are offered as dwarfs. Clapp's Favorite is recommended as hardy for cooler regions, and ripens in mid- to late-August.
   A five-in-one pear tree grafted onto fairly hardy rootstock is now offered by Burpee. The varieties are Kieffer, Bartlett, Favorite, Seckle and Beurre Bosc.

PLUMS: An old-fashioned fruit not seen too often in today's gardens, the plum is one of the most decorative of the fruit trees when in bloom. It is a small tree, well-suited to the home garden. Burbank is one dwarf variety offered. It bears reddish-purple plums in August and reaches no more than 8 to 9 feet at maturity. In standard sizes, Burbank also is offered. Shropshire Blue Damson produces large crops of dark-purple fruit in early August. Damson won't cross-pollinate Burbank, which must be pollinated by a Stanley or a Fellenburg plum, usually offered by Burbank dealers. A good pollinator is Abundance, which bears bright-red fruit in August.

PLANTING AND CULTURE

General instructions for planting orchard fruit trees appear in Chapter Four. Specific instructions are included with the tree you purchase. It is a good idea to give a young fruit tree protection from drying winter winds the first year, if you can. It is really important that it be well watered the first year it is in the ground. The second year, it will be established and can be watered when you water the shrubs in the garden. In early spring the third year, scratch a general fertilizer in around the base of the tree to encourage production. Weeds at the foot of an established tree don't harm it. A lot of big weeds at the foot of a very young tree can absorb water and food the plants will need, so keep the weeds to a minimum around young plantings.

ORCHARD TREES IN CONTAINERS

Orchard fruit trees growing in containers require more watering than those growing in the ground. The nutrients in the soil must be replenished more often, too, since the roots can't go foraging for food or water beyond the walls of their containers. The third year your tree has been growing in its container, remove the top 5 or 6 inches of soil and replace it with new soil, well-supplied with organic matter and fertilizer.

BRAMBLE FRUITS

VARIETIES TO CONSIDER

BLACKBERRIES: Blackberries require a mild climate and should be considered only if you have space to spare. The flavor of ripe blackberries, just picked, is delicious, but not as much of a world-wide favorite as that of raspberries. A good all-purpose blackberry is Eldorado. Darrow bears over a long period, and is excellent for jellies, as well as for eating fresh. Bailey ripens its fruit in August, and Thornfree, a new introduction from the USD, lives up to its name, and has no thorns.

BLUEBERRIES: Blueberry bushes do well in foundation plantings where acid-loving evergreens flourish. They can be fertilized with an evergreen fertilizer suited to rhododendrons and azaleas. The only thing to consider before loading your foundation planting with blueberries, is whether you are going to be willing to cover the fruits with netting to keep the birds from beating you to the harvest. If you are, then consider either the high-bush (tall) or low-bush varieties. Plant two or more varieties for cross-pollination. Blueray is an early type that ripens fruit usually in July. Earliblue ripens fruit in June in most areas. Rancocas is a midseason variety, and Jersey late variety.

RASPBERRIES: Raspberries of one variety or another flourish all over North America, even in very cool zones. Black and red raspberry varieties are offered by most dealers in both standard and everbearer types. September Everbearer Red, and Gold, bear a first crop in June and a second crop in September. Heritage reverses the process. It bears a modest crop of berries in summer and a big crop in September. Indian Summer is another fall everbearer. Latham, a red raspberry, and Cumberland, a black, are standard raspberries that produce excellent crops once during the season.

PLANTING AND CULTURE

General instruction for planting bramble fruits appear in Chapter Four. Specific instructions are furnished by dealers with each plant. The rules that apply for watering the orchard trees the first season, apply to the bramble fruits as well. Fertilize bramble fruits in early spring the third season. Fertilize the everbearers a second time, shortly before the second crop is due to appear.

GRAPES: A GOOD CHOICE FOR THE SMALL GARDEN

Grapes grow well in containers. The roots take little space and the branches can be trained in any direction. They are an excellent choice as a fruit crop for the small garden. Time was

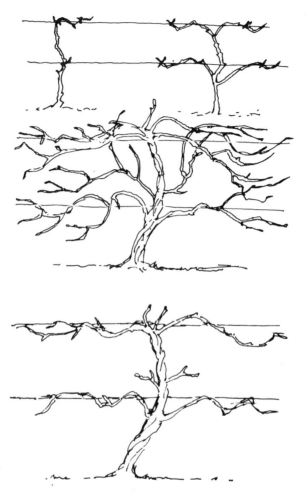

*Kniffen pruning system for grapes shows grape bush staked to
horizontal wires and pruned back at the end of the first season;
grape pruned back at the end of the second season; growth that
takes place in third season; third season growth pruned back.
The four long lead canes of the third season growth have been
pruned back to an inch beyond 12 buds each; four short canes
have been pruned back to the first bud on each. It is on these
short stubs that the canes will develop that will be next season's
lead canes. Fruit grows on the branches from the long canes.*

when in the North the only variety that survived the climate was Concord, bearing small grapes superb for jelly-making and not too wonderful for eating. Today that isn't so: Captivator, a red grape, Seedless Interlaken, a green grape, and Steuben, a black grape, are among eating grapes offered as hardy. Of the three, Seedless Interlaken is claimed to be the hardiest. Growing grapes for wine-making requires more space than most really small gardens offer. Grapes are sold by catalogs and garden supply centers usually as balled and burlapped plants.

PLANTING AND CULTURE

Plant grapevines early in spring, in holes larger than the roots, and about 15 inches deep, so that only a few buds appear on the part of the stem remaining above ground. Containers for grapes should be 24 inches deep and 2 feet square at least. Soil should be sandy, and very well drained, with a good supply of organic matter. At the end of the growing season, when the plant is about to become dormant, remove all top growth, leaving only one or two of the strongest canes. Train these on horizontal wires, as shown in the sketch. Or, run them up the sides of an arbor, or along trellising pegged to a wall with a southwestern exposure, or on any high-rise structure that will be attractive in your garden. Fertilize the soil lightly early in spring the third year. Grapes do best in somewhat infertile soils.

SPRAYING SCHEDULES FOR FRUIT

Organic gardeners avoid spraying their fruit trees. I have tried that and found it wanting. More particularly, the trees ended up wanting fruit, and so did I. For most urban and suburban gardeners, some spraying, preferably with a nontoxic product, is necessary. Ask the local Agricultural Extension Service for recommendations for sprays for fruit plants in your area. Follow the manufacturers' instructions

171

very carefully. Combination sprays have been made to handle both diseases and pests that attack fruit plants. They save multiple sprayings.

APPLES AND PEARS: Plan on six sprayings: the first when the buds show pink, but before the blooms open; the second as soon as the petals have fallen; the third, 10 days later; the four, 2 weeks later; the fifth, 2 weeks after that; the sixth, 2 weeks after that.

PEACHES AND NECTARINES: Plan six sprayings. First spraying should be in early spring while the plant is still dormant; second spraying, as soon as the petals have fallen; the third, 10 days later; the fourth, 2 weeks later; the fifth, 2 weeks later; the sixth, 6 weeks later. This last spraying won't be needed for early varieties.

PLUMS AND CHERRIES: Plan to spray four times. The first spraying takes place as soon as the petals have fallen; the second, 10 days later; the third, 1 week later; the last, 2 weeks later. Skip this one for early varieties of cherry.

STRAWBERRIES: Generally, they won't need spraying. However, you'll have to find a way to protect the fruit from the birds, unless you want to share it. Birds have a way of poking holes in beautiful berries that would be less distressing if they'd take the whole berry. I use netting to protect ripening crops.

RASPBERRIES, BLACKBERRIES, BLUEBERRIES: Like strawberries, they generally don't require spraying of the sort indicated for the orchard fruits. However, you will need netting to protect the ripening fruit from the birds, or one morning you'll wake up ready to harvest and find the crop all gone, or halfgone and half spoiled.

GRAPES: Grapes require spraying in most areas, five times. Spray when new growth is 12 inches long. Spray again when the shoots are 12 inches long. Spray again 1 week after blooming. Spray again 3 weeks later. Spray again 4 weeks before the harvest is due.

Part IV

PROBLEMS THAT ATTACK
FOOD PLANTS

Chapter Ten

KEEPING THE GARDEN HEALTHY

Organic gardeners talk a lot about how well-prepared, fertile soils seem to produce plants much more immune to pests and diseases than do poor, arid soils. So the first step in a program to protect your plants against the problems that beset them is to give them good soil to grow in. (See Chapter Three.) Keeping the garden mulched and damp through droughts helps plants stay healthy and strong enough to resist problems.

Occasionally you will hit trouble spots, and the information below suggests ways to handle them. In applying any of the remedies recommended here, remember that you are spraying food, not flowers, and follow the manufacturers instructions closely.

There are other things you can do to ward off food plant problems.

PROVIDE A GOOD AIR CIRCULATOR

Plants growing too closely together tend to stay damp after rain or watering: prolonging humidity, especially when the weather is hot, breeds trouble. Don't water on muggy days; in such weather, the plants have trouble throwing off moisture, and may become subject to diseases.

175

PRACTICE CROP ROTATION

Many of the plants that go into the food garden are related; tomatoes and eggplants and potatoes, for instance, are related, as are cabbage, cauliflower, and broccoli, and cucumbers, squashes, and melons. It stands to reason that pests or diseases that love one plant will also enjoy a close relative if it is the next set into that piece of ground. For this reason, gardeners practice crop rotation for those plants most susceptible to pests and diseases. Another reason to alternate crops is that plants tend to take particular ingredients from the soil leaving it poor in those ingredients. To follow one plant with a near relative is to plant in soil that probably lacks important nutrients even if the soil has been well fertilized. Farmers and professional growers pay a great deal of attention to rotating their crops, and so should you.

DISCARD OLD OR DISEASED PLANTS

Plants most susceptible to diseases (cabbage, cucumbers, for instance) should be discarded as soon as their crops have been harvested, even if the plants are healthy. Left to rot in their rows, they may attract or foster the very pests and diseases you've been successful in keeping away while the plants were growing. Dispose of such discards in the compost pile if you have one—as long as they are healthy. If they are diseased, burn them if possible, but don't in any case add them to the compost.

CONSIDER DISEASE-RESISTANT VARIETIES

Most catalogs offer varieties of each food plant that have been developed to resist the most common diseases associated with the plants. These are not always the best varieties, though generally, breeders try to breed resistance into their best varieties. If any of the diseases common on the following chart are rampant in your area, look for and buy disease-resistant varieties for your own garden.

KEEPING FURRY FRIENDS AWAY

The average small garden is set in a civilized spot, where lovely furry friends like rabbits and deer aren't likely to be. However, if you run into trouble—rabbits nibbling all the seedlings, for instance—try spreading dried blood, sold by most garden centers as a supplier of nitrogen, where the animals cause damage. It keeps them away. A fenced-in garden isn't as pretty as an open one, but it does keep most creatures from treating it as a larder. A good mouser and a noisy aggressive dog are perhaps the best deterrents to the type of garden-raider you are apt to run into.

FIGHTING PROBLEMS THE ORGANIC WAY

A whole book can be written—and many have been—on the subject of keeping pests and diseases away without the use of even the sensible chemicals recommended in the chart below. It's a science—not always an exact one—but one that has some merit.

To sum it up in a nutshell, strong, smelly plants like herbs and flowers such as marigold, set around plants susceptible to common diseases, do seem to offer some protection. I loaded my garden in Westport, Connecticut, for about four years running with every conceivable kind of marigold, and eventually I felt I had far less of every little, bad, creeping, crawly thing than had been there before.

Edging the food garden or food plants in containers with dwarf African marigolds, herbs, nasturtiums, garlic, or onions may offer real protection, and can be pretty as well as useful. Encouraging the presence in the garden of the natural foes of your plant enemies is another organic approach. Birds eat insects which eat plants and spread diseases among them. To encourage birds, leave a brambly, natural patch where they can nest and feel safe from cats, and plant bushes and ornamental fruit trees that bear berries birds eat. Import—you can buy them from catalogs—and protect the insects that prey on insects that do damage to plants. The praying mantis, the lacewing, ladybird beetles, ground beetles, and tiger beetles are the best known.

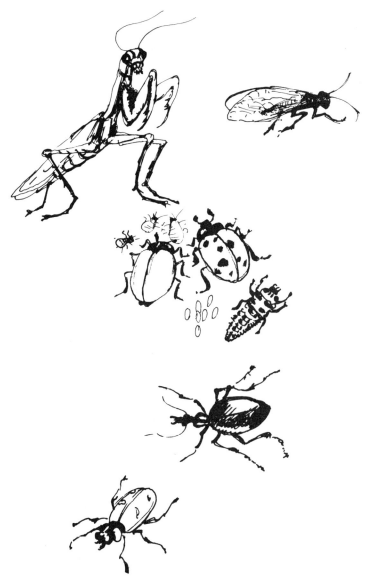

Garden helpers: good guys from the insect world. Clockwise from top: praying mantis, adult lacewing, ladybird beetles, ladybird larvae, ladybird eggs, ground beetle, tiger beetle.

COMMON VEGETABLE PROBLEMS AND THE SOLUTIONS

ASPARAGUS

Rust: The ferns have a yellow, spiky look. The solution is to plant resistant varieties and burn the plants in early autumn.

Beetle: New shoots are eaten away. Dust with Rotenone during the harvest season, and with Methoxychlor after harvest.

BEANS

Anthracnose: Sympthoms are dark, sunken, round spots, pink in the center, that appear on the pods. The solution is to use Western seed. Do not touch the plants when they are wet.

Bacterial blight: The symptoms are brown areas on the leaves, and red-brown spots on the pods. Solution is as above.

Mosaics: Symptoms are the yellow mottling of the leaves, and stunted plants. Solutions are to plant resistant varieties, and to control the aphids that spread the disease with Malathion.

Mexican bean beetle: Leaves are eaten away to skeletons. Control the beetles with Rotenone dust.

Bean weevil: Symptom is round holes in the dried beans after they have been stored. Solution: spray plants next year with Bordeaux Mixture, Ziram, or Zeneb.

Downy mildew: The bean pods show white mold. Treat the plants weekly with Maneb or Zineb.

BEETS

Leaf spot: The symptoms are brown spots that dry and leave holes. Treat with Bordeaux Mixture, Ziram, or Zineb.

Aphids: Symptoms are small green lice on the leaves, especially the undersides, and leaves that become dwarfed and deformed. Dust with Nicotine.

BRASSICAS: CABBAGE, CAULIFLOWER, BRUSSELS SPROUTS, BROCCOLI

Black rot: The symptoms are plants that yellow, brown, then die. The solution is to rotate the crops next time. Never plant a member of the brassica crop where another brassica was the previous crop.

Club root: The plants wilt, and the dug-up roots turn out to be malformed. The solution, again, is crop rotation. Check the soil pH, too, and make sure it is between 6.0 and 7.0.

Yellows: Symptoms are dwarfed plants with yellowed lower leaves that drop off. The solution is to plant disease-resistant varieties.

Cabbage worms: The symptoms are nasty green caterpillars, and foliage that shows signs of having been eaten. The solution is to dust with Rotenone.

Cutworms: The symptoms are wiry, small brown worms. The solution is to set out poisoned bait sold by garden supply centers.

CARROT

Leaf blight: The symptoms are yellow or brown spots on the leaves and tops that die away. The solution is to use Maneb or Zineb four or five times at 10-day intervals, starting when the plants are 6 inches tall.

Yellows: The centers of the leaves yellow. The solution is to control leafhoppers which spread the disease with Malathion or Carbaryl.

CELERY

Early blight: Leaves show small yellow spots that turn gray. Plant treated seeds next time; meanwhile use Maneb or Zineb every 7 days.

Late blight: The older leaves will have small brown spots that develop black dots. Treat as early blight.

Tarnished plant bug: A mottled brown bug appears and the stalks show symptoms of their gnawing. Control the bugs with Malathion or Rotenone.

CORN

Corn smut: The plants show silver or gray swellings that puff out black spores at maturity. The solution is to burn the swellings before maturity. If you have corn smut, be sure to rotate the crops every second or third year and plant only resistant varieties.

Bacterial wilt: The symptoms are leaves with light green or yellow streaks and plants that are stunted or that wilt. Control the flea beetles that carry the disease with Carbaryl by spraying before the seedlings appear. Also, use resistant varieties in your garden.

Corn borer: The symptoms appear only after the ears have been harvested—ears with holes bored in them. Next year, use Carbaryl on the plants when half the corn silk shows.

Corn earworm: Silk and tips show signs of having been eaten. The solution is to treat the silk with Carbaryl as it emerges, and to repeat the treatment three times at 2-day intervals.

CUCURBITS: CUCUMBER, SQUASH, MELONS, PUMPKINS

Anthracnose: Symptoms are sunken spots on the fruit, which are pink at first and then turn black. The solution is to use treated seed next time and to rotate crops. Treat affected plants with Captan or Maneb at 7- to 10-day intervals beginning when the plants are seedlings.

Downy mildew: A grayish fungus appears on the undersides of the leaves. Use only resistant varieties next time, and treat, as above, with Maneb.

Powdery mildew: The symptoms are powdery gray-white growths on the leaves and leaves that fall off. To correct, spray with Karathane when the mildew first appears, and repeat 10 days later.

Bacterial wilt: The leaves turn dull and wilt, and the plant dies. Treat with Rotenone.

Striped cucumber beetle: Foliage is eaten. Control the beetles with Carbaryl Malathion or Methoxychlor.

EGGPLANT

Verticillium wilt: Symptoms are leaves that turn yellow, then brown, and stunted plants. Solution is to change the location of the garden, or, if that isn't practical, not to plant eggplant there again, or tomatoes.

Phomopsis blight: The young plants are covered with brown spots and the seedlings rot at ground level. Next time, use treated seed. Treat with Maneb or Captan weekly.

Flea beetle: Symptoms are tiny holes in the leaves. The solution is to spray at weekly intervals with Carbaryl or Rotenone.

LETTUCE

Bottom rot and drop rot: The plants rot at the base and the rot eventually spreads to the tops. Damp, heavy soil is often the cause, so change the planting to a well-drained location and rotate the location of the lettuces in your garden at each planting. Don't mulch your lettuces if you are having difficulties with rot.

Leafhoppers: The leaves are chewed and the heads become deformed. Treat with Carbaryl, Malathion, or Methoxychlor as soon as the seedlings appear.

ONIONS

Pink root: Symptoms are stunted plants, many of which die; you'll see the evidence in onions that turn pink, then black. Use resistant varieties and do not plant onions where evidence of the disease has appeared.

Downy mildew: The tops of the leaves have pale green spots, and the plants turn yellow. Treat with Maneb or Zineb.

Thrips: Leaves at the neck of the bulb are eaten. Apply Malathion often.

PARSLEY

Crown rot: A soft rot that spreads. Practice crop rotation.

PEAS

Root rot: The stems decay and the plant dies. Plant resistant varieties next time; practice crop rotation; plant only in well-drained soil.

Aphids: Small green lice appear and the leaves become dwarfed. Dust with Nicotine.

Ascochyta blight: Symptoms are gray areas with brown dots on the peapods and on the leaves of the plant. Practice crop rotation and plant only disease-resistant varieties next time.

PEPPERS

Bacterial leaf blight: Leaves show raised yellow spots. Next time, plant resistant varieties and practice crop rotation.

Phoma rot: Fruits show water-soaked areas which enlarge and blacken. Solution is to practice crop rotation.

Blossom end rot: Fruit bottoms show dark-brown sunken areas. Cause can be too much nitrogen fertilizer and an uneven water supply. Correct.

Aphids: Undersides of leaves have soft insects. Dust with Malathion.

Mites or red spider: Leaves show small white spots where tiny pale, or reddish, insects have fed. Solution is to dust with Malathion.

POTATOES

Early blight: Foliage shows dark brown circular spots. Treat with Zineb and plant only healthy tubers.

Late blight: Evidence is water-soaked areas. Solution is as above.

Rhizoctonia: Tubers show a dark fungus growth. Avoid this in future planting by setting out only disease-free or treated seeds or tubers.

Scab: Tubers show corky scabs on the skin. Usually a result of soil that is too alkaline. Correct.

Potato beetle: Leaves have reddish larvae and later striped bettles with brown markings appear. Treat with rotenone.

TOMATOES

Blossom end rot: Fruit bottoms show dark brown sunken area. Maintain even moisture through the growing season and avoid the use of a highly nitrogenous fertilizer.

Fusarium wilt: The lower leaves wilt and then yellow and die. Plant only resistant varieties and use crop rotation.

185

Leaf roll: Leaves are rolled up. This doesn't affect yield—so ignore it.

Catface: The fruit has a cat-like formation at the lower end. The cause is unknown. The USDA suggests as a solution that you plant only varieties recommended by local garden centers.

Early blight: Irregular, brown, target-like pattern of spots. Treat with Maneb every 5 to 7 days during the growing season.

Late blight: Greenish-black blotches that are dark and look water-soaked. Solution is Maneb every 5 to 7 days.

Anthracnose: Water-soaked spots on the fruit. Stake the plants, and apply Maneb weekly beginning when the plants first bloom.

Horn worm: A large, hideous green caterpillar appears and eats the leaves and the fruit. Carbaryl applications will dispose of it. If you see one, pick it off into a jar of foam detergent, and look for and dispose of any others that may be there. They do a great deal of damage in a very short time.

Mites or red spiders: Small white spots appear on the leaves. Apply Malathion to the undersides of the leaves.

Flea beetle: Leaves show tiny black holes. Treat with Carbaryl or Rotenone at weekly intervals.

ASK THE AGRICULTURAL EXTENSION SERVICE FOR HELP

If you are uncertain of the identities of problems plaguing your crops, send samples of the affected plants to the local Agricultural Extension Service. They'll identify the trouble, and suggest solutions.

APPENDIX

ADDRESSES OF STATE AGRICULTURAL
EXTENSION SERVICES

Alabama Polytechnic Institute, Auburn, Alabama
University of Alaska, College, Alaska
University of Arizona, Tucson, Arizona
College of Agriculture, University of Arkansas, Fayetteville, Arkansas
College of Agriculture, University of California, Berkeley, California
Colorado State University, Fort Collins, Colorado
College of Agriculture, University of Connecticut, Storrs, Connecticut
Connecticut Agricultural Experiment Station, New Haven, Connecticut
School of Agriculture, University of Delaware, Newark, Delaware
University of Florida, Gainesville, Florida
College of Agriculture, University of Georgia, Athens, Georgia
University of Hawaii, Honolulu, Hawaii
University of Idaho, Moscow, Idaho
College of Agriculture, University of Illinois, Urbana, Illinois
Purdue University, Lafayette, Indiana
Iowa State College of Agriculture, Ames, Iowa
Kansas State College of Agriculture, Manhattan, Kansas
College of Agriculture, University of Kentucky, Lexington, Kentucky

Agricultural College, Louisiana State University, Baton Rouge, Louisiana
College of Agriculture, University of Maine, Orono, Maine
University of Maryland, College Park, Maryland
College of Agriculture, University of Massachusetts, Amherst, Massachusetts.
College of Agriculture, Michigan State University, East Lansing, Michigan
Institute of Agriculture, University of Minnesota, St. Paul, Minnesota
Mississippi State College, State College, Mississippi
College of Agriculture, University of Missouri, Columbia, Missouri
Montana State College, Bozeman, Montana
College of Agriculture, University of Nebraska, Lincoln, Nebraska
College of Agriculture, University of Nevada, Reno, Nevada
University of New Hampshire, Durham, New Hampshire
Rutgers University, New Brunswick, New Jersey
College of Agriculture, State College, New Mexico
College of Agriculture, Cornell University, Ithaca, New York
State College of Agriculture, University of North Carolina, Raleigh, North Carolina
State Agricultural College, Fargo, North Dakota
College of Agriculture, Ohio State University, Columbus, Ohio
Oklahoma A. and M. College, Stillwater, Oklahoma
Oregon State College, Corvallis, Oregon
Pennsylvania State University, University Park, Pennsylvania
University of Puerto Rico, Box 607, Rio Piedras, Puerto Rico
University of Rhode Island, Kingston, Rhode Island
Clemson Agricultural College, Clemson, South Carolina
South Dakota State College, College Station, South Dakota
College of Agriculture, University of Tennessee, Knoxville, Tennessee
Texas A. and M. College, College Station, Texas
College of Agriculture, Utah State University, Logan, Utah
State Agricultural College, University of Vermont, Burlington, Vermont
Virginia Polytechnic Institute, Blacksburg, Virginia
State College of Washington, Pullman, Washington
West Virginia University, Morgantown, West Virginia

College of Agriculture, University of Wisconsin, Madison, Wisconsin

College of Agriculture, University of Wyoming, Laramie, Wyoming

Index

Agricultural Extension Service, 35, 51, 53, 186-189
air circulation, 175
ammonium nitrate, 73
ammonium sulfate, 54
animal and insect garden helpers, 177-179
anise, 159
apples, 165-166
apples, crab, 166
artichoke, Jerusalem, 96-97
artichokes, 117-119
asparagus, 82-84

basil, 159
baskets, hanging, 17-18
beans, 119-121
beets, 84-86
blackberries, 168
blueberries, 168
borage, 159
bramble fruits, planting, 70
broccoli, 86-88
Brussels sprouts, 88-89

cabbage, 89-90
caraway, 159
carrots, 90-91
catnip, 160
cauliflower, 92
celeriac, 121-122
celery, 122-123
chard, 93
cherries, 166
chervil, 160
chicory, 94

chives, 160
clay, 50
climbers, 16-17
compost, 51, 55-57
container gardens, 41-42
coriander, 160
corn, 123-125
cress, 95
crop
  early, 64
  late, 64
  midseason, 64
crop rotation, 176
cucumbers, 125-126

dandelions, 96
"dictionary of food plants," 77-172
dill, 160
diseased plants, discarding, 176
disease-resistant plants, 176
diseases and remedies, 180-186

early spring planting rule, 79
  exceptions to, 80
eggplant, 145-146

fennel, 160
"fertilizers, complete," 53
flats, seedlings in, 72-75
flower border, planning a, 42-46
fruit plants
  "balled-and-burlapped," 69
  "bare-root," 69
  buying, 65
  maturing of, 35-36
fruits, bramble, 168-169